Freedom of Speech
on
Private Property

Recent Titles from Quorum Books

Freedom of Speech on Private Property

WARREN FREEDMAN

QUORUM BOOKS

New York · Westport, Connecticut · London

323,443
F85f

Library of Congress Cataloging-in-Publication Data

Freedman, Warren.
 Freedom of speech on private property / Warren Freedman.
  p. cm.
 Bibliography: p.
 Includes index.
 ISBN 0-89930-323-4 (lib. bdg. : alk. paper)
 1. Freedom of speech—United States. 2. Right of property—United
States. I. Title.
KF4772.F74 1988
346.7304—dc19
[347.3064]   87-32262

British Library Cataloguing in Publication Data is available.

Library of Congress Catalog Card Number: 87-32262
ISBN: 0-89930-323-4

First published in 1988 by Quorum Books

Greenwood Press, Inc.
88 Post Road West, Westport, Connecticut 06881

Printed in the United States of America

The paper used in this book complies with the
Permanent Paper Standard issued by the National
Information Standards Organization (Z39.48-1984).

10 9 8 7 6 5 4 3 2 1

Contents

Acknowledgments

It would be a travesty if the author did not acknowledge the special "contributions" of the Law Library of Pace University School of Law in White Plains, New York, and of the Law Library of the University of Connecticut School of Law in Hartford. The availability of these facilities for research made this writing a joyful experience.

Then, too, acknowledgment is justified for the help and assistance of my loving wife, Esther Rosenbluth Freedman; the advice of my son-in-law, Michael S. Stiebel, Esq., a practicing attorney in Hartford, Conn.; and the understanding of my children: Mrs. Deborah Freedman Stiebel of Avon, Conn., my son Dr. Douglas Freedman of Yonkers, N.Y., and my daughter, Ms. Miriam Freedman of New York City.

Preface

The First Amendment guarantee of freedom of speech is meaningless unless one can exercise that right on public property as well as on private property, and recognition of this postulate is at the heart of this single volume of constitutional law. But there are restrictions on the exercise of this fundamental right of free speech, as set forth particularly in Chapter 2. These restrictions or limitations embrace what is politely delineated as "private property," an amorphous concept that constantly demands re-definition. The role of the states is important, for there the Fourteenth Amendment comes into play (as described in Chapter 4); equal treatment before the law and due process of the law are the subjects of Chapters 4, 5, and 6.

Chapter 7 delves into "commercial speech" and defines its protection under the First Amendment. Chapter 8 takes on the militant topic of billboards and political advertising with resulting restrictions, while Chapter 9 is concerned with the pragmatics of picketing, pamphleteering, petitioning, electioneering, and the right to demonstrate—all viewed from the catbird seat of the First Amendment. The final chapter opens up the discussion of sex and the First Amendment; pornography, prostitution, obscenity, and ethnic, racial, and other offensive slurs are all examined in terms of their lack of protection under the First Amendment. There are also sections on cable television and, finally, a parting glimpse at English law on First Amendment practices.

The author submits that this single volume, touching so many bases of First Amendment protection, answers the question of how First Amendment protection can be meaningfully extended to public and to private property. Where courts hem in this fundamental right of freedom of speech, in whatever its form, the constitutional plague is upon all other fundamental rights of the person.

Freedom of Speech
on
Private Property

Introduction to Freedom of Speech Generally

Congress shall make no law . . . abridging the freedom of speech, or of the press; or the right of the people peaceably to assemble, and to petition the government for a redress of grievances.

This First Amendment to the U.S. Constitution delineates, inter alia, guarantees of particular fundamental rights of speech, of press, of assembly, and of the right to petition. It was in Marsh v. Alabama[1] that the U.S. Supreme Court observed that "the right to exercise the liberties safeguarded by the First Amendment lies at the foundation of free government by free men." Three years later, in 1949, the highest court, in Terminiello v. City of Chicago,[2] recognized the vital role of the First Amendment.

The vitality of civil and political institutions in our society depends on free discussion. . . . It is only through free debate and free exchange of ideas that government remains responsive to the will of the people and peaceful change is effected. The right to speak freely and promote diversity of ideas and programs is therefore one of the chief distinctions that set us apart from totalitarian regimes.[3]

The framers of the Bill of Rights and the U.S. Constitution knew that a person burdened with an idea or program has a need, even a moral duty, to express it; and a thinking person can experience no greater affront to his or her humanity than denial of that freedom of expression. Liberty of expression benefits more than the speaker; the listener, the viewer, and the reader suffer a violation of their fundamental liberty if they are denied access to the ideas or programs of other persons.[4] Liberty to express an idea or program is essential to the pursuit of truth, to the power of reason, and to the ultimate human perfectibility. The 1979 case of United States

v. Progressive, Inc.[5] is a fitting example of this relentless search for truth fostered by the First Amendment. Here the defendant, a magazine, purported to disclose in lay terms the secret of the hydrogen bomb design, despite the ban on publication or disclosure of information useful in the manufacture of nuclear weapons, under the Atomic Energy Act of 1954[6]. The federal district court in Wisconsin issued an injunction forbidding the publication, but the government soon abandoned the suit when it became plain that the secret information was already available in other publications. The Seventh U.S. Court of Appeals dismissed the appeal, intimating that the statutory prohibition of freedom of expression was vulnerable to challenge under the First Amendment as a barrier to the free pursuit of scientific knowledge.[7]

The First Amendment embraces both freedom of speech and freedom of the press, but these freedoms are not necessarily coextensive. Justice Potter Stewart opined in 1975 that "the Free Press guarantee is, in essence, a structural provision of the Constitution"[8] and as such confers substantive rights not available under the free speech guarantee. History casts little light on whether freedom of the press differs from freedom of speech. As of 1978, Chief Justice Warren Burger acknowledged that the U.S. Supreme Court "has not yet squarely resolved whether the Press Clause confers upon the 'institutional press' any freedom from government restraint not enjoyed by others."[9] Yet the duality suggests that a separate press clause implies that speech via the press might be subject to some restraints that would not be applicable to other speech. There is indeed the concept of the "responsible" press; that is, newspapers, publications, motion pictures, radio, and television broadcasts have a certain undefined responsibility in the exercise of their First Amendment rights to act responsibly in their public roles.[10]

Alexander Meiklejohn, the American philosopher of freedom of expression,[11] contended that the guarantees of freedom of speech and freedom of the press hold an absolute, preferred position because they are measures adopted by the people as the ultimate rulers in order to retain political control over governmental processes. As Justice William Brennan explained in Garrison v. Louisiana,[12] "Speech concerning public affairs is more than self-expression; it is the essence of self-government." And seven years later in 1971 in Cohen v. California,[13] Justice John Harlan explained: "The constitutional right of free expression . . . is designed and intended to remove governmental restraints from the arena of public discussion, putting the decision as to what views shall be voiced largely in the hands of each of us, in the hope that use of such freedom will ultimately produce a more capable citizenry and more perfect polity and in the belief that no other approach would comport with the premise of individual dignity and choice upon which our political system rests."[14]

But freedom of speech or of expression, despite its political primacy, can never be absolute. In times of war or similar crisis, the survival of the nation may be at stake, and restrictions on freedom of speech are inevitable. Defamatory statements are actionable at the instigation of the defamed, and impugning the integrity of a court by publishing evidence in advance of trial may jeopardize the administration of justice; therefore such efforts must be restrained. Public safety may take precedence over freedom of expression, although the states are still bound under the Fourteenth Amendment[15] to respect the guarantees of the First Amendment. The First Amendment, despite restrictions, is at the very core of the United States and its democratic life.[16] As illustrated in Hall v. May Department Stores Co.,[17] where an employee brought an action for damages for defamation and intentional infliction of emotional distress allegedly suffered after she was questioned by store security personnel about shortages in the cash register, the Oregon Supreme Court ruled that the accusations of the store security personnel were "speech and expression of opinion" within the meaning of the First Amendment, guaranteeing the right to speak, write, or print freely on any subject whatever, subject to legal responsibility for the abuse of this right.[18]

If freedom of speech or expression is important in a democracy,[19] then speakers or those exercising that right must have access to places where people congregate so that the right may be exercised. Streets, sidewalks, parks, and other similar public places are readily available, as demonstrated by such decisions of the U.S. Supreme Court as Hague v. Congress of Industrial Organizations[20] and Food Employees Local v. Logan Valley Plaza, Inc.[21] But socioeconomic changes have shifted the focus of community life from these traditional public forums to privately owned forums, such as shopping centers, airports, and corporate office complexes. To bar reasonably expressive behavior on private property, it is submitted, diminishes the validity of the guarantee of free speech as set forth in the First Amendment. And yet the First Amendment bars only the federal government and the state governments [under the Fourteenth Amendment] from abridging free speech; private acts of abridgement are not prohibited by the First Amendment.

1.1 PRINCIPLE OF EQUAL RESPECT

Inherent within the definition of freedom of speech or of expression is the principle of equal respect that democratic peoples demonstrate for one another in "the exercise of the moral powers fundamental to their status as sovereigns over themselves and the State."[22] Equal respect in principle means that one person does not exercise the right of freedom of speech, for example, at the expense of another person's right to be secure in person and property, as where the former calls out "fire!" in a crowded theater or where the former insists on exercising the right of free speech in the living room of the latter's private home. Professor Richards in his book *Toleration and the Constitution* cited as a disturbed example of this principle of equal respect the U.S. Supreme Court decision in Buckley v. Valeo.[23] At stake was the constitutionality of the Federal Election Campaign Act of 1971 as amended, which imposed limitations on the amounts that could be contributed to presidential campaigns and the amounts that could be spent on such campaigns by candidates and by independent groups in behalf of such candidates. The thrust of the act was admittedly anticorruption, although equalizing political power among the candidates seemed to be the true purpose of the act. The highest court legitimized contribution to campaign limitations since campaign limitations did not inhibit freedom of speech or of expression. But the Court struck down the expenditure limitations because expenditure limitations inhibited free speech interests without deterring the corruptive influences. In short, a restriction on presidential campaign expenditures, as opposed to contributions, was termed to be a diminution of speech.

As the Court expressed it, "The concept that government may restrict the speech of some elements of our society in order to enhance the relative voice of others is wholly foreign to the First Amendment, which was designed to 'secure the widest possible discrimination of information from diverse and antagonistic sources.' "[24] The right of free speech is a right of equality, a like liberty for all, even though economic and associated inequalities frequently undercut the background quality of equal respect inherent in the First Amendment. Thus, the regulation by the federal government of electoral expenditures in the interest of equalizing political power should not be regarded as antagonistic to the values of the First Amendment: "The diminution in speech activity from expenditure limits is not a content-biased restriction on speech condemned by free speech jurisprudence."[25] It is a reasonable attempt to effect the underlying constitutional ideal of equal respect.

1.2 GOVERNMENT ABRIDGEMENT OF FREEDOM OF SPEECH

Professor Laurence H. Tribe, in *American Constitutional Law*,[26] pointed out that government can abridge freedom of speech by (1) taking aim at ideas or information for control or penalty, as illustrated by governmental punishment of publications critical of the government[27] or by governmental ban on the teaching of a foreign language,[28] and (2) constricting the flow of information and ideas, as illustrated by enforcing rules, compliance with which would discourage the communication of ideas or information.[29] Both aspects of government abridgement of freedom of speech have adverse effect on communicative opportunity, which is at the very heart of the First Amendment.[30] As the U.S. Supreme Court in Police

Department of the City of Chicago v. Mosely[31] observed, "Government has no power to restrict expression because of its message, its ideas, its subject matter, or its content."

Governmental action may not ban all distribution of handbills in order to combat litter,[32] but government may bar noisy demonstrations on public streets abutting schools when classes are in session.[33] Government may not, as shown in Virginia State Board of Pharmacy v. Virginia Citizens Consumer Council, Inc.,[34] prohibit advertising of drug prices by pharmacists because the public's right to know is superior to the plaintiff's effort to maintain high professional standards among pharmacists who might be jeopardized by price wars. The balancing of interests here means that noncommunicative impacts may more readily be regulated by government than communicative impacts. If communicative impacts are to be regulated, there must be convincing proof of "clear and present danger,"[35] for example. In United States v. O'Brien,[36] the highest court upheld the conviction in the late 1960s of a young man who on the steps of the courthouse in Boston burned his draft card to protest the war in Vietnam; it was a felony knowingly to destroy or mutilate a draft card. The Court opined that the statute furthered the legitimate interest of the federal government in maintaining the efficient operation of the draft. But in State of West Virginia v. Barnette,[37] schoolchildren could not be required to join in a flag salute ceremony; forcing people to express a view is as offensive as forbidding them to express a view.

Historically, government abridgement of freedom of speech revolved about the law of seditious libel. In 1806, the U.S. government commenced common law prosecutions of six citizens of Connecticut for seditious libel against President Thomas Jefferson.[38] According to the indictments, two defendants had committed the crime of sedition in the course of preaching, and four defendants had committed the crime of sedition in newspaper print.[39] Since the infamous Sedition Act of 1798 had expired, the federal prosecution was based upon the common law crime of seditious libel. Politics intervened, and the Jefferson administration dropped the charges against the preachers but continued the prosecution of two editors of the Federalist newspaper in Hartford, Connecticut.[40] Although the case was appealed directly to the U.S. Supreme Court, no decision was handed down until 1812 when the Supreme Court, dominated by Republicans, ruled that there was no such federal law of crime. This bizarre prosecution did not speak well for Jeffersonian democracy, which sought to quell opposition, despite the strictures of the First Amendment that there shall be no law abridging the freedom of speech or press. Fortunately, the Sedition Act of 1798 was generally held to be invalid; there was "principled opposition" to seditious libel on the part of the public.[41] Freedom of speech then had the common law meaning of freedom to speak, write, and publish as one pleased subject to subsequent punishment for being too offensive. President Jefferson in 1788 had opined: "A declaration that the federal government will never restrain the presses from printing any thing they please will not take away the liability of printers for false facts printed."[42] Obviously the truth is a defense at all times.[43]

In June 1987 at the bicentennial celebration of the U.S. Constitution in Philadelphia, federal government officials endeavored to ban from the federally owned mall protesters who opposed the Reagan administration on U.S. involvement in Nicaragua. But federal district court judge John P. Fullam observed that government officials who controlled the Independence Mall "may not fully appreciate the reach of the First Amendment" for they had violated the free speech rights of the protesters. The court accused the federal government of seeking "to prevent plaintiffs from expressing their dissenting views in any manner which might come to the attention of persons attending the Vice President's speech and which might detract from the mainstream patriotism reflected by the We the People 200 insignia."[44]

About the same time the U.S. Supreme Court unanimously struck down a ban on solicitation imposed by the Los Angeles Board of Airport Commissioners, which had decided that the airport was "not open for First Amendment activities by any individual or entity." The highest court viewed the ban as unconstitutional on its face because its scope was so broad. But the Court did not determine whether the airport terminal was a conventional public forum open to freedom of expression or a specialized place like government buildings or military bases where it is reasonable to impose certain limits on freedom of expression.[45]

Another interesting observation is that the First Amendment restraint upon Congress to "make no law . . . abridging the freedom of speech, or of the press" may not have necessarily included the states; indeed, it is argued that "a primary purpose of the First Amendment was to reserve to the States an exclusive authority to legislate in the field of speech and press."[46]

1.3 PUNITIVE DAMAGES: A DETERRENT TO FREEDOM OF SPEECH

The U.S. Supreme Court in 1964 in New York Times Co. v. Sullivan[47] expressed the conviction that fear of libel suits and accompanying punitive damages had a "chilling effect" upon the free expression of diverse opinion, even though the court's ruling on "actual malice" was confined to public figures and public officials who, in in order to recover damages for libel, must prove that the statement was made either with knowledge that it was false or with reckless disregard of whether it was false. Punitive damages ipso facto constitute a deterrent to freedom of speech, as set forth by the highest court in 1974 in Gertz v. Robert Welch, Inc.,[48] which held that punitive damages in libel actions contravened the guarantees of the First Amendment in cases in which the plaintiff failed to prove "constitutional malice" (that is, the subjective awareness of falsity), unless there was some fault on the part of the defendant.[49] In short, the only speech on matters of public concern that may be subject to punitive damages is speech spoken or written with "constitutional malice." However, the Oregon Supreme Court in Wheeler v. Green[50] in 1979 banned punitive damage awards based upon the freedom of the press clause in the state constitution. The dissent of Justice Harlan in Rosenbloom v. Metromedia, Inc.[51] argued that the chilling effect of punitive damages was so great that punitive damages could never be awarded consistently with the guarantee of freedom of the press.

It is said that punitive damages are awarded for purposes of deterrence, retribution, and compensation.[52] Punitive damages in civil actions deters antisocial conduct or behavior that is not serious enough to be punished criminally.[53] The 1967 case of Curtis Publishing Co. v. Butts[54] illustrates the deterrence purpose; the highest court upheld punitive damages of $460,000 (reduced from $3 million) against a nationally distributed magazine for libel. The magazine unsuccessfully argued that the power to award punitive damages gave the jury the power to destroy a publisher's business through excessive awards. In his dissent in the 1971 Rosenbloom case,[55] Justice Thurgood Marshall warned that "fear of extensive awards" would necessarily curtail a free flow of opinion in the news media and thereby frustrate First Amendment policy. He also observed that punitive damages gave unsympathetic juries a tool to punish unorthodox and unpopular opinions. The second purpose of retribution is seldom expressed as a ground for punitive damages, but it is often the motive behind the punitive damages award.[56] If this is true, then the criminal safeguards under the Constitution must be guaranteed, and that takes the civil case out of the usual procedural safeguards that fall behind in severity criminal safeguards.[57] Yet in Beauharnais v. State of Illinois,[58] the U.S. Supreme Court upheld a conviction for criminal libel as constitutional, despite the retributive features of the Illinois statute, which prohibited public dissemination of statements derogatory of a racial group. The third purpose, compensation, is not served by imposing punitive damages and has a chilling effect on First Amendment values. Awarding of attorneys' fees within the concept of punitive damages makes no sense, for these fees are within the discretion of the court unless otherwise mandated by statute.

1.4 THE DEFENSE OF THE FIRST AMENDMENT

Negligent publishing and negligent broadcasting instances have focused attention upon the defense of the First Amendment. In Walt Disney Productions, Inc. v. Shannon,[59] a child suffered personal injury by imitating a stunt he saw on the television show "Mickey Mouse Club." A participant on the show had demonstrated how to reproduce the sound of a tire coming off an automobile by putting a BB pellet inside a large balloon, filling the balloon with air, and rotating the BB inside the balloon. The child tried to imitate the stunt; he blew up a balloon with a BB inside, but the balloon burst and propelled the BB into his eye, partially blinding him. Suit was brought against the producer, syndicator, and broadcaster, and the Georgia trial court granted defendant's motion for summary judgment. The Georgia Supreme Court affirmed, holding that since the television show did not come within any of the categories of "unprotected speech," the show did not create a clear and present danger of an immediate breach of the peace, and therefore there could be no liability as a matter of law. In the same year, 1981, in Olivia N. v. National Broadcasting Co., Inc.,[60] the California appellate court entertained a suit brought by the victim of a crime who identified the specific NBC program that had allegedly incited the group sexual assault upon the plaintiff. But the court applied the First Amendment defense, for otherwise a contrary result would lead to "self-censorship which would dampen the vigor and limit the variety of public debate."

In Demuth Development Corp. v. Merck & Co., Inc.,[61] plaintiff was the manufacturer of an air sterilization appliance used in hospitals and by other firms requiring a germ-free environment. Plaintiff alleged that the defendant, publisher of the "Merck Index," implied that the principal ingredient in the plaintiff's product, triethylene glycol, was a hazardous and toxic substance because the defendant had cross-referenced the chemical with ethylene glycol, which was toxic. The federal court in New York dismissed the suit on the basis that the defendant publisher owed no legal duty to the plaintiff:

But even if we assume that Merck was under a duty to its *readers* to provide such information with care, how does that help plaintiff? Plaintiff does not and could not claim it relied to its detriment on misinformation published by Merck. Nor does plaintiff point to any "relationship between the parties, arising out of contract or otherwise," which "in morals or good conscience," place Merck under any duty towards plaintiff or its business. On the contrary, Merck's right to publish is guaranteed by the First Amendment . . . and the overriding societal interest in the untrammeled dissemination of knowledge. The right is circumscribed by laws such as those respecting national secrets, copyright, obscenity, defamation, and unfair competition. The court has already held that no claim for defamation is stated and plaintiff does not rely on any grounds other than negligence and wilful misrepresentation.[62]

This defense of the First Amendment precludes tort liability, for example, for the negligent activity of publishing or broadcasting. Otherwise the tort liability would have a chilling effect upon the freedom of expression or even suffocate free expression as protected by the First Amendment. However, it might be difficult to justify extension of the First Amendment defense to insulate a publisher or a broadcaster from liability where there has indeed been a clerical error, such as mistakenly depicting the location of a television tower on a map (an error that caused an aircraft to strike a guy wire supporting the tower).[63] The First Amendment serves no purpose in immunizing a publisher or broadcaster or mapmaker from a clerical error under circumstances causing grievous bodily injury or substantial property damages or loss.[64]

A bizarre and difficult problem of speech confrontation of a public employee reached the U.S. Supreme Court in 1987 in Rankin v. McPherson.[65] Here a nineteen-year–old clerical employee in a county constable's office, upon hearing of the attempt to assassinate President Reagan, remarked to her co-worker boyfriend, "If they go for him again, I hope they get him."[66] Unknown to Miss McPherson, her casual remark was overheard by another employee in the same office, and the county constable thereupon fired her. Her statement was made during a private conversation in a private room not open to the public. The Court by a 5–4 vote ruled that the firing violated her First Amendment rights:

> It is clearly established that a State may not discharge an employee on a basis that infringes that employee's constitutionally protected interest in freedom of speech. *Perry* v. *Sindermann*, 408 U.S. 593, 597 (1972). Even though McPherson was merely a probationary employee, and even if she could have been discharged for any reason or for no reason at all, she may nonetheless be entitled to reinstatement if she was discharged for exercising her constitutional right to freedom of expression. See *Mt. Healthy City Board of Education* v. *Doyle*, 429 U.S. 274, 284–285 (1977); *Perry* v. *Sindermann, supra*, at 597–598.
>
> The determination whether a public employer has properly discharged an employee for engaging in speech requires "a balance between the interests of the [employee], as a citizen, in commenting upon matters of public concern and the interest of the State, as an employer, in promoting the efficiency of the public services it performs through its employees." *Pickering* v. *Board of Education*, 391 U.S. 563, 568 (1968); *Connick* v. *Myers*, 461 U.S. 138, 140 (1983). This balancing is necessary in order to accommodate the dual role of the public employer as a provider of public services and as a government entity operating under the constraints of the First Amendment. On one hand, public employers are *employers*, concerned with the efficient function of their operations; review of every personnel decision made by a public employer could, in the long run, hamper the performance of public functions. On the other hand, "the threat of dismissal from public employment is . . . a potent means of inhibiting speech." *Pickering*, 391 U.S., at 574. Vigilance is necessary to ensure that public employers do not use authority over employees to silence discourse, not because it hampers public functions but simply because superiors disagree with the content of employees' speech.

The majority opinion of Justice Marshall continued:

The statement was made in the course of a conversation addressing the policies of the President's administration. It came on the heels of a news bulletin regarding what is certainly a matter of heightened public attention: an attempt on the life of the President. While a statement that amounted to a threat to kill the President would not be protected by the First Amendment, the District Court concluded, and we agree, that McPherson's statement did not amount to a threat punishable under 18 U.S.C. §871(a) or 18 U.S.C. §2385, or, indeed, that could properly be criminalized at all. See 786 F. 2d, at 1235 ("A state would . . . face considerable constitutional obstacles if it sought to criminalize the words that were uttered by McPherson on the day the President was shot"); see also Brief for United States as *Amicus Curiae* 8 ("we do not think that respondent's remark could be criminalized"); cf. *Watts* v. *United States*, 394 U.S. 705 (1969) (*per curiam*). The inappropriate or controversial character of a statement is irrelevant to the question whether it deals with a matter of public concern. "[D]ebate on public issues should be uninhibited, robust, and wideopen, and . . . may well include vehement, caustic, and sometimes unpleasantly sharp attacks on government and public officials." *New York Times Co.* v. *Sullivan* 376 U.S. 254, 270 (1964); see also *Bond* v. *Floyd*, 385 U.S. 116, 136 (1966): "Just as erroneous statements must be protected to give freedom of expression the breathing space it needs to survive, so statements criticizing public policy and the implementation of it must be similarly protected."

The concurring opinion of Justice Powell did not expend time on balancing the public employee's interest in commenting on "matters of public concern" against the State's interest in running an efficient public service;[67] he doubted that "a single, offhand comment directed to only one other worker will lower morale, disrupt the workforce, or otherwise undermine the mission of the office." But the scathing dissent of Justice Scalia (joined by Chief Justice Rehnquist, and Justices White and O'Connor) stated that he did not "look forward to the new First Amendment world the Court creates, in which nonpolicy-making employees of the Equal Opportunity Commission must be permitted to make remarks on the job approving of racial discrimination."

That McPherson's statement does not constitute speech on a matter of "public concern" is demonstrated by comparing it with statements that have been found to fit that description in prior decisions involving public employees. McPherson's statement is a far cry from the question by the assistant district attorney in *Connick* whether her co-workers "ever [felt] pressured to work in political campaigns," *Connick*, at 149; from the letter written by the public school teacher in *Pickering* criticizing the board of education's proposals for financing school construction, *Pickering*, at 566; from the legislative testimony of a state college teacher in *Perry* v. *Sindermann*, 408 U.S. 593, 595 (1972), advocating that a particular college be elevated to 4-year status; from the memorandum given by a teacher to a radio station in *Mt. Healthy City Board of Ed.* v. *Doyle*, 429 U.S. 274, 282 (1977), dealing with teacher dress and appearance; and from the complaints about school board policies and practices at issue in *Givhan* v. *Western Line Consolidated School Dist.*, 439 U.S. 410, 413 (1979). See *Connick*, at 145–146.

McPherson's statement is indeed so different from those that it is only one step removed from statements that we have previously held entitled to no First Amendment protection even in the nonemployment context—including assassination threats against the President (which are illegal under 18 U.S.C. §871), see *Frohwerk* v. *United States*, 249 U.S. 204, 206 (1919); " 'fighting' words," *Chaplinsky* v. *New Hampshire*, 315 U.S. 568, 572 (1942); epithets or personal abuse, *Cantwell* v. *Connecticut*, 310 U.S. 296, 309–310 (1940); and advocacy of force or violence, *Harisiades* v. *Shaughnessy*, 342 U.S. 580, 591–592 (1952). A statement lying so near the category of completely unprotected speech cannot fairly be viewed as lying within the "heart" of the First Amendment's protection; it lies within that category of speech that can neither be characterized as speech on matters of public concern nor properly subject to criminal penalties, see *Connick*, at 147. Once McPherson stopped explicitly criticizing the President's policies and expressed a desire that he be assassinated, she crossed the line.

The Court reaches the opposite conclusion only by distorting the concept of "public concern." It does not *explain* how a statement expressing approval of a serious and violent crime—assassination of the President—can possibly fall within that category. It simply rehearses the "context" of McPherson's statement, which as we have already seen is irrelevant here, and then concludes that because of that context, and because the statement "came on the heels of a news bulletin regarding what is certainly a matter of heightened public attention: an attempt on the life of the President," the statement "plainly dealt with a matter of public concern." *Ante*, at 7. I cannot respond to this progression of reasoning except to say I do not understand it. Surely the Court does not mean to adopt the reasoning of the court below, which was that McPherson's statement was "addressed to a matter of public concern" within the meaning of *Connick* because the public would obviously be "concerned" about the assassination of the President. That is obviously untenable: The public would be "concerned" about a statement threatening to blow up the local federal building or demanding a $1 million extortion payment, yet that kind of "public concern" does not entitle such a statement to any First Amendment protection at all.[68]

NOTES

1. 326 US 501 (1946) at p. 509.
2. 337 US 1 (1949).
3. Id. at p. 10. Also see generally 10 Golden Gate U L Rev 805 (1980).
4. See Scanlon, "A Theory of Freedom of Expression," 1 Philos & Pub Aff 204 (1972), and 94 Harv L Rev 1 (1980).
5. 467 F Supp 990 (WD Wis., 1979), app dism 610 F2d 819 (7th Cir., 1979).
6. 42 USC 2011-96 (1976).
7. Id.
8. Stewart, "Or of the Press," 26 Hastings L J 631 (1975).

9. First National Bank of Boston v. Bellotti, 435 US 765 (1978) at pp. 797–98.

10. See generally 7 Hofstra L Rev 595 (1979).

11. Meiklejohn, Free Speech and Its Relation to Self-Government (1948) and Political Freedom (1960).

12. 379 US 64 (1964).

13. 403 US 15 (1971); also infra note 4 at p. 3.

14. Id. at p. 14.

15. The First Amendment has been held to be incorporated into the Fourteenth Amendment since Gitlow v. New York, 268 US 652 (1925).

16. See generally 9 Emory L J 59 (1986).

17. 292 Ore 131, 637 P2d 126 (1981).

18. Similarly, in Rankin v. McPherson, 786 F2d 1233 (5th Cir., 1986), the federal appellate court upheld the employee's utterance as protected by the First Amendment. Here a clerk-typist in the office of the county constable in Houston, Texas, wished aloud for President Reagan's death when John Hickley, Jr., shot the president; she was promptly fired. She successfully sued the constable and the county for reinstatement and for back pay. The court agreed, pointing out that the constable's distaste at continuing her employment pales in importance to the free speech rights of the employee; also the clerk-typist should not be denied First Amendment protection because the government's interest in promoting employee morale, although significant, is still outweighed by First Amendment issues.

19. See generally 46 Alb L Rev 1501 (1982). Also, note Emerson, The System of Freedom of Expression 6–7 (1970).

20. 307 US 496 (1939).

21. 391 US 308 (1968).

22. See Richards, Toleration and the Constitution (Oxford University Press, 1986) at pp. 215 et seq.

23. 424 US 1 (1976).

24. Id. at pp. 48–49.

25. Infra note 22 at p. 218.

26. (1978) at Section 12–2.

27. See New York Times Co. v. Sullivan, 376 US 254 (1964) at p. 276.

28. See Meyer v. Nebraska, 262 US 390 (1923).

29. See Kovacs v. Cooper, 336 US 77 (1949).

30. Note, 88 Harv L Rev 1482 (1975); also infra note 25.

31. 408 US 92 (1972) at pp. 95–96.

32. See Schneider v. Sate, 308 US 147 (1939).

33. See Grayned v. City of Rockford, 408 US 104 (1972).

34. 425 US 748 (1976).

35. See generally 22 Stan L Rev 1163 (1970).

36. 391 US 367 (1968).

37. 319 US 624 (1943).

38. See Levy, Jefferson and Civil Liberties (1963) at pp. 61–66.

39. See generally 32 UCLA L Rev 177 (1984).

40. Note Smith, Freedom's Fetters (1956), at pp. 188–200.

41. Infra note 38 at p. 181.

42. Id. at p. 191.

43. See Letter to Madison, July 31, 1788, printed in 13 Papers of Thomas Jefferson 442 (Boyd ed., 1950).

44. See New York Times (July 11, 1987) at p. 10.

45. See New York Times (June 22, 1987) at pp. B1 et seq.

46. Infra note 39 at p. 207.

47. Infra note 27.

48. 418 US 323 (1974).

49. See Garrison v. Louisiana, 379 US 64 (1964).

50. 593 P2d 777 (Ore., 1979).

51. 403 US 29 (1971) at pp. 72–78. See generally 45 Fordham L Rev (1977) at pp. 1382 et seq.

52. See 45 Fordham L Rev (1977) at pp. 1386 et seq.

53. See 70 Harv L Rev 517 (1957) at p. 523.

54. 388 US 130 (1967).

55. Infra note 51.

56. See 41 NYS L Rev 1158 (1966) at pp. 1161–62.

57. See 44 Harv L Rev 1173 (1931) at p. 1177.

58. 343 US 250 (1952).

59. 276 SE2d 580 (Ga., 1981).

60. 126 Cal App3d 488 (1981).

61. See Reminga v. United States, 631 F2d 449 (6th Cir., 1980).

62. Id. at p. 993.

63. 432 F Supp 990 (EDNY, 1977).

64. See generally 64 Va L Rev 1123 (1978), and Pearlman and Marks, "Broadcast Negligence: Television's Responsibility for Programming," Trial Magazine (August 1980) at pp. 43–44.

65. 107 S Ct 2891 (1987).

66. According to the Court,

On March 30, 1981, McPherson and some fellow employees heard on an office radio that there had been an attempt to assassinate the President of the United States. Upon hearing that report, McPherson engaged a co-worker, Lawrence Jackson, who was apparently her boyfriend, in a brief conversation, which according to McPherson's uncontroverted testimony went as follows:

"Q: What did you say?

"A: I said I felt that that would happen sooner or later.

"Q: Okay. And what did Lawrence say?

"A: Lawrence said, yeah, agreeing with me.

"Q: Okay. Now, when you—after Lawrence spoke, then what was your next comment?

"A: Well, we were talking—it's a wonder why they did that. I felt like it would be a black person that did that, because I feel like most of my kind is on welfare and CETA, and they use medicaid, and at the time, I was thinking that's what it was.

" . . . But then after I said that, and then Lawrence said, yeah, he's cutting back medicaid and food stamps. And I said, yeah, welfare and CETA. I said, shoot, if they go for him again, I hope they get him."

McPherson's last remark was overheard by another deputy constable, who, unbeknownst to McPherson, was in the room at the time. The remark was reported to Constable Rankin, who summoned McPherson. McPherson readily admitted that she had made the statement, but testified that she told Rankin, upon being asked if she made the statement, "Yes, but I didn't mean anything by it." App. 38. After their discussion, Rankin fired McPherson.

McPherson brought suit in the United States District Court for the Southern District of Texas under 42 U.S.C. §1983, alleging that petitioner Rankin, in discharging her, had violated her constitutional rights under color of state law. She sought reinstatement, back pay, costs and fees, and other equitable relief. . . .

67. See generally A.B.A.J. (December 1, 1987) at 48 et seq.
68. The dissent concluded as follows:

In sum, since Constable Rankin's interest in maintaining both an esprit de corps and a public image consistent with his office's law enforcement duties outweighs any interest his employees may have in expressing on the job a desire that the President be killed, even assuming that such an expression addresses a matter of public concern it is not protected by the First Amendment from suppression. I emphasize once again that that is the issue here— and *not*, as both the Court's opinion and especially the concurrence seem to assume, whether the means used to effect suppression (viz., firing) were excessive. The First Amendment contains no "narrow tailoring" requirement that speech the government is entitled to suppress must be suppressed by the mildest means possible. If Constable Rankin was entitled (as I think any reasonable person would say he was) to admonish McPherson for saying what she did on the job, within hearing of her co-workers, and to warn her that if she did it again a formal censure would be placed in her personnel file, then it follows that he is entitled to rule that particular speech out of bounds in that particular work environment—and that is the end of the First Amendment analysis. The "intemperate" manner of the permissible suppression is an issue for another forum, or at least for a more plausibly relevant provision of the Constitution.

Because the statement at issue here did not address a matter of public concern, and because, even if it did, a law enforcement agency has adequate reason not to permit such expression, I would reverse the judgment of the court below.

First Amendment: Restrictions on Freedom of Speech

2.1 TIME, PLACE, AND MANNER OF EXPRESSION

The First Amendment gives speech and related forms of expression virtually absolute protection against restrictions, except where public safety and public security are endangered. In New York Times Co. v. United States,[1] involving the threatened publication of the so-called Pentagon Papers in 1971, the federal government argued that publication would increase the risk of injury to national interests, including the deaths of soldiers, the destruction of military alliances, difficulties in negotiation with enemies, inability of diplomats to communicate, and prolongation of the war in Vietnam. But the highest court ruled that these allegations would not support an injunction against publication. In condemning prior restraints, Justice Brennan opined: "Only the governmental allegation and proof that publication must inevitably, directly, and immediately cause the occurrence of an event kindred to imperiling the safety of a transport already at sea can support even the issuance of an interim restraining order."[2] Yet in the 1980 decision of Snepp v. United States,[3] where a former Central Intelligence Agency (CIA) agent sought to publish a surreptitiously obtained account of CIA activities in South Vietnam, the same court affirmed portions of the judgment adverse to Snepp and also reversed the portion of the judgment adverse to the United States.[4] Here, Snepp's publication was not only the breach of a binding contract but a shabby violation of a personal confidence voluntarily accepted.[5] On the other hand, the restrictions here undoubtedly violated the citizenry's right to know about the conduct of its government. As expressed in First National Bank v. Bellotti,[6] the First Amendment does have a role "in affording the public access to discussion, debate, and the dissemination of information and ideas."[7] In Landmark Communications, Inc. v. Virginia,[8] the highest court set aside the conviction of a newspaper publisher for accurately reporting the status of an official Virginia judicial inquiry in violation of a Virginia statute that declared that the proceedings were confidential. In upholding no restriction upon free speech and free press, the Court asserted that the commonwealth of Virginia had failed to prove that the publication gave rise to a clear and present danger of interference with the administration of justice.[9] And yet here the person who revealed the confidential information to the press could be punished, but not the newspaper publisher who caused the real harm by publishing what it had been told unlawfully under Virginia law.

In most instances, the states regulate the time, place, and manner of expression.[10] In Lovell v. City of Griffin,[11] the U.S. Supreme Court had in 1938 established a guideline for state courts with respect to freedom of expression where a license was necessary to demonstrate or otherwise express a particular conviction: a law requiring a license must explicitly confine the licensing authorities to considerations of traffic control, crowd control, and other public safety considerations. It was in Cohen v. California[12] that the court upset the conviction of a young man for wearing a shirt emblazoned with "Fuck the Draft": "The First and Fourteenth Amendments must be taken to disable the States from punishing public utterance of this unseemly expletive in order to maintain what they regard as a suitable level of discourse within the body politic."[13] Indeed, the task of accommodation in public places is singularly difficult because gross offense to sensibilities usually results from obscene words that are but a vehicle of expression or speech protected under the First Amendment.

It was in 1964 that the U.S. Supreme Court in New York Times Co. v. Sullivan[14] astounded the press by proclaiming that the First Amendment bars a state from awarding a public official damages for a defamatory falsehood relating to his or her official conduct unless the falsehood was published with knowledge of its falsehood or with reckless disregard for its truth or falsity. This expansion upon the importance of freedom of the press and of speech gave the press the incentive to embark upon investigations into corruption, conflicts of interests, and other abuses of public trust in government, without the fear of having to pay damages to a public person whom they might injure by publishing what some jury later finds to be false and defamatory.

But "a State or municipality may protect individual privacy by enacting reasonable time, place, and manner regulations applicable to all speech irrespective of content. But when the government, acting as censor, undertakes selectively to shield the public from some kinds of speech on the ground that they are more offensive than others, the First Amendment strictly limits its power."[15] But explicitly sexual or scatological speech is only "second-class" speech and not entitled to First Amendment protection, as illustrated in the case of regulations of the Federal Communications Commission (FCC) against a radio station in FCC v. Pacifica Foundation.[16]

In general, it may be said that a state may place reasonable time, place, and manner restrictions on speech without regard to content, provided that the speech takes place in the public forum. In Linmark Associates, Inc. v. Township of Willingboro[17] the highest court invalidated a ordinance banning "for sale" and "sold" signs for the purpose of stemming the flight of white home owners from a racially integrated township because the ordinance was concerned with content of speech. Similarly, in Saia v. New York,[18] the same court almost thirty years earlier had invalidated a city ordinance that forbade the use of sound amplifiers on trucks without the permission of the chief of police. The uncontrolled discretion of the chief of police was an infringement on free speech, for it related to the content of speech. A city ordinance that prohibited the business practice of soliciting magazine subscriptions door to door without prior invitation of the home owner may not infringe upon First Amendment rights.[19] But where the city ordinance forbade any person to knock on doors, ring doorbells, or otherwise summon any resident to the door for the purpose of receiving handbills or other distribution, the Court knocked down the ordinance, as in Martin v. Struthers,[20] as "invalid because in conflict with the freedom of speech and press."[21] The ordinance made the trespasser a criminal for entering the premises without any explicit command from the house owner to stay away; furthermore, the Court was aware that door-to-door businesses are "essential to the poorly financed causes of little people."[22]

In State of Oregon v. Harrington,[23] the Oregon appellate court was concerned about the constitutionality under the Oregon Constitution of a state statute[24] that provides that "a person commits the crime of harassment if, with intent to harass, annoy, or alarm another person, the actor . . . publicly insults another by abusive or obscene words or gestures in a manner likely to provide a violent or disorderly response."[25] The court found the statute "was intended to protect the listener from exposure to abusive or obscene language rather than to protect anyone from physical violence." Furthermore, the Oregon Constitution forbade any state statute "restricting the right to speak freely on any subject whatever." Abusive language cannot be curbed by an outright prohibition but can be thwarted by a civil suit for damages. Abusive, vulgar, or offensive speech is protected under the First Amendment,[26] even though such protection might invite abuses in other areas such as law enforcement where prosecutors and police may be the objectives of such abusive, vulgar and offensive speech.[27]

Time, place, or manner of expression restrictions may be invoked under licensing statutes such as the one involved in Lovell v. Griffin,[28] where the defendant, a member of Jehovah's Witnesses, was convicted for distributing religious tracts in violation of a city ordinance forbidding the distribution unless a permit was first procured from the city. The U.S. Supreme Court held the ordinance invalid on its face as a prior restraint, and therefore the defendant had no need even to apply for a permit. On the other hand, in Poulos v. New Hampshire,[29] the defendant was convicted for holding a religious service in a public park without a proper license. The defendant had applied for a license but was denied one, and the New Hampshire trial court found the ordinance to be a reasonable restriction of the time, place, and manner of speech in public places. The highest state court affirmed, as did the U.S. Supreme Court, which upheld the ordinance as a reasonable licensing statute: "To allow applicants to proceed, without the required permits, to . . . hold public meetings without safety arrangements or take other unauthorized action is apt to cause breaches of the peace or create public dangers. . . . Delay is unfortunate, but the expense and annoyance of litigation is a price citizens must pay for life in an orderly society where the rights of the First Amendment have a real and abiding meaning."[30] However, according to the Court, a state may generally make an unlawful refusal to license a defense to a licensing statute.[31] But if the licensing statute is invalid, the refusal to license is of no legal consequence; if the licensing statute is valid on its face, a defense of failure to apply for a license because the license is not available is not allowed.[32]

2.2 THE POLICE POWER

The police power of the federal government may be seen in the action against freedom of speech and of the press in the 1984 U.S. Supreme Court decision of Regan v. Time, Inc.[33] The defendant magazine published a photograph in color of a copy of a U.S. monetary obligation or other security in violation of 18 U.S. Code 474, a criminal statute designed during the Civil War to combat counterfeiting caused then by the increase in federal government monetary obligations issued to fund the war. According to the highest court, "Compliance with these requirements does not prevent Time, Inc. from expressing those views," but it was unnecessary for the magazine to violate the criminal statute in doing so. Thus, federal police power held sway over the First Amendment rights here.

The city of New York in 1986 brought an action for an injunction directing defendant to remove sidewalk bins through which defendants distributed free of charge their *Learning Annex Magazine*, which described courses offered by defendants. Defendants in City of New York v. American School Publications, Inc.[34] pointed out that the city allows other publications to set up similar but coin-operated newspaper vending machines; the city replied that defendant's publication was an advertisement and not a publication and consequently could not be distributed through sidewalk bins. But the New York Court of Appeals did not agree with the city's contention: "The City's arguments miss its central handicap in this case—a government official or employee may not exercise complete and unregulated discretion, in the absence of duly enacted guidelines or procedures, to decide which publications may be distributed via bins installed on city streets. We agree that the City may regulate the installation of bins on its sidewalks, but it must do so by properly drawn regulations synchronizing the City's right to maintain health and safety with First Amendment speech and press freedoms." The highest New York court continued:

First Amendment guarantees have been extended to the means of distributing a newspaper as well as to content. . . . Moreover, the right of access to public streets and sidewalks, subject to appropriate regulation, is essential to the exercise of First Amendment freedom, and the right of access includes the right to distribute printed materials. . . . First Amendment protection, however, does not exempt newspaper or magazine dispensing bins from all government regulation. The Constitution does not guarantee the right to communicate views at all times, in all places, or in any manner that an individual desires. . . . Newsbins, like billboards[35] and many other means of communication, involve both communicative and noncommunicative aspects. . . . While the government may have a legitimate interest in regulating noncommunicative aspects of the media, it is also restricted from interfering with the communicative aspects. Government is compelled, therefore, to reconcile its regulatory interest with the First Amendment interest at stake.

The New York Court of Appeals concluded:

The Constitution recognizes a municipality's interest under the police power to ensure the safe and reasonably smooth flow of pedestrian movement on its streets and even the effort at relative cleanliness of its streets. However, First Amendment freedoms are implicated in the recognition of those interests. In order to exert its policy power and to restrict access to a public forum, a municipality must adopt reasonable regulations governing the time, place, and manner of expression. The regulations must be content neutral, sensitively calibrated to the governmental interest at stake, and must also leave open alternative channels of communication. . . . They must be publicly promulgated upon being duly enacted.[36]

The U.S. Supreme Court in Houston v. Hill,[37] decided in June 1987, struck down a Houston ordinance that made it a crime to "interrupt" police officers in the pursuit of their work: "We are mindful that the preservation of liberty depends in part upon the maintenance of social order. . . . But the First Amendment recognizes, wisely we think, that a certain amount of expressive disorder not only is inevitable in a society committed to individual freedom, but must itself be protected if that freedom would survive." Two months earlier, the federal district court for the Southern District of New York in Rock Against Racism v. Ward[38] carefully scrutinized police regulations for use of Central Park in New York City for a politically motivated band concert. The court found the guidelines not to violate plaintiffs' First Amendment rights to the extent that the guidelines require use of a city-contracted amplification system, the imposition of a $50 to $100 permit fee, the requirement of a reasonable cleanup bond, the imposition of time limitations on amplified sound, and the imposition of vehicle permits. However, the court found the following police guidelines to be unconstitutional: imposition of a $100 per hour user fee for the amplification system; imposition of an insurance requirement that vested unfettered discretion in the City Parks Department; unreasonable limitation on the size of the audience; unreasonable time durational requirements for certain events; and the prohibition on solicitation of funds and revenue.

A state's police power may be invoked in the face of First Amendment demands. The essence of the police power is that "the deprivation of individual rights cannot prevent its operation."[39] Subordination of an individual's rights to the rights of society at large is a necessary corollary of the police power.[40] Reasonable restrictions upon the exercise of freedom of speech are consistent with the exercise of state police power.[41] In the landmark case of Robins v. Pruneyard Shopping Center,[42] the California court echoed the conclusion that individual rights are subject to the limitation that they may not be used in a way inimical to the public interest. The court relied upon state police power as authority for the California regulation on shopping centers, thereby providing common law protection against the shopping center's abridgement of plaintiff's First Amendment rights. Under police power, private property interests must yield to zoning laws, environmental needs, and other public concerns.[43] Protecting freedom of speech is on par with protection of "health and safety, the environment, aesthetics, property values, and other societal goals that have been held to justify restriction on private property rights."[44]

2.3 ZONING REGULATIONS

Courts have traditionally examined zoning ordinances that have the effect of restricting freedom of speech and of expression. In Heffron v. International Society for Krishna Consciousness, Inc.,[45] the Court faced defendant's religious ritual, which required its members to distribute and sell religious literature and to solicit donations. The local zoning ordinance prohibited the "sale or distribution of any merchandise, including printed or written material," as well as solicitation of funds, except from a duly licensed booth on the fairgrounds. The court upheld the zoning ordinance as a reasonable time, place, and manner regulation not violative of the First Amendment or the Fourteenth Amendment; furthermore, the regulation was not based on the content or the subject matter of the speech or expression, not discriminatory in that the method of allocating space at the fair was not open to arbitrary application, and served a significant governmental interest due to the state's need to maintain the orderly movement of peoples on the fairgrounds.[46]

In Schad v. Mount Ephraim,[47] a local zoning regulation banned all live entertainment in a commercial zone. An adult bookstore desired to operate a coin machine that allowed the viewer to see a live nude dancer performing behind a panel. The U.S. Supreme Court invalidated the zoning regulation upon the ground that the manner of expression, live entertainment, was incompatible with activities normally allowed in a commercial zone. Furthermore, "To be reasonable, time, place or manner restrictions not only must serve significant State interests but also leave adequate alternative channels of communication." Indeed the zoning regulation did not leave adequate alternative channels of communication because it totally banned live entertainment.

The city of San Diego had a comprehensive zoning regulation that banned outdoor display signs subject to important restrictions such as on-site signs and twelve other categories. Several outdoor advertising companies attacked the zoning ordinance in Metromedia, Inc. v. City of San Diego,[48] a case in which the U.S. Supreme Court wrote five separate opinions. The majority view upheld the zoning law insofar as it regulated commercial speech but found a portion of the law to be violative of First Amendment rights. The law had allowed commercial on-site signs but had discriminated against noncommercial on-site signs by banning them. Furthermore, the zoning regulations were not a reasonable time, place, or manner restriction because the regulations had completely banned the noncommercial on-site signs based upon content; that is, their content was noncommercial. A majority of the Court was also of the opinion that the city of San Diego had not shown adequate justification for its assertion that billboards had actually impaired traffic safety.[49] The three dissenters agreed that the zoning regulation was constitutional, and Justice William Rehnquist opined that the aesthetic justification for the zoning regulation was sufficient to sustain the zoning regulation. Chief Justice Burger in his dissent urged that the federal courts here had shown a "long arm and voracious appetite . . . with a vengeance, reaching and absorbing traditional concepts of local authority."

That same year, 1981, also saw a decision by the Texas Civil Court of Appeals in Houston Chronicle Publishing Co. v. City of Houston.[50] Five years earlier, the defendant had enacted an ordinance that made it "unlawful for any person to sell or offer for sale any newspaper to any occupant of any vehicle which is in a street or on other public property, whether or not such vehicle is moving, stopped or parked, and whether or not the person selling or offering for sale such newspaper is, or is not, on a public street or on public property." The sweep of the Houston ordinance prompted the plaintiff, a newspaper publisher, to enjoin its enforcement, but the district court found the ordinance to be constitutional. The Texas appellate court reversed, saying the ordinance was overbroad on its face and abridged the right of free speech by curtailing circulation of published material.[51] The Texas appellate court recognized that access to public streets or circulation of the material was essential to First Amendment freedoms.[52] On the other hand, traffic control and public safety were legitimate exercises of the state's police power.[53] The court balanced the "diverse legitimate interests" and came away with the view that the Houston ordinance "sweeps too broadly, unnecessarily invading appellant's protected freedoms."[54] The court refused to snuff out First Amendment rights, despite the city's legitimate effort to keep youthful hawkers of newspapers off congested city streets. The Texas Supreme Court in the same year in Iranian Muslim Organization v. City of San Antonio[55] had reiterated that a permissible regulation could not be used as a guise to suppress freedom of speech. Indeed, a state may not place restrictions on the use of newspaper vending machines on sidewalks;[56] a state may not prevent door-to-door canvassing and distribution of leaflets;[57] and a state may not prevent the passing out of handbills to passersby.[58]

The U.S. Supreme Court for fifty years has shown little tolerance for suppression of free speech under the guise of legitimate regulation.[59] In 1981, the highest court in the Heffron case[60] invalidated regulations that appeared facially neutral but lent themselves to arbitrary application and potential suppression of dissident views.[61]

2.4 SYMBOLIC SPEECH

The concept that speech may be nonverbal or expressive was recognized by the U.S. Supreme Court in the 1981 decision in Stromberg v. California.[62] A state statute prohibited the displaying of a red flag "as a sign, symbol or emblem of opposition to organized government." The statute was found to be unconstitutional on the grounds that its language was so vague as to permit punishment for the fair use of "the opportunity for free political discussion."[63] Symbolic speech was given First Amendment protection thirteen years later in West Virginia Board of Education v. Barnette[64] when the highest court struck down a state statute mandating that public school children must salute the flag even if the act of saluting is in violation of their religious beliefs: "No official . . . can proscribe what shall be orthodox in politics, nationalism, religion, or other matters of opinion, or force citizens to confess by word or act their faith therein."[65] But twenty-five years later, in United States v. O'Brien,[66] the highest court viewed the burning of a draft card as not symbolic speech: "We cannot accept the view that an apparently limitless variety of conduct can be labeled 'speech' whenever the person engaging in the conduct intends thereby to express an idea."[67] Accordingly, the Court spelled out four factors for determining when government regulation of expressive conduct is warranted: (1) "if it is within the constitutional power of Government"; (2) "if it furthers an important or substantial governmental interest"; (3) "if the governmental interest is unrelated to the suppression of free expression"; and (4) "if the incidental restriction on alleged First Amendment freedoms is no greater than is essential to the furtherance of that interest."[68]

The wearing of black armbands in school to symbolize objection to the Vietnam War was upheld, however, in Tinker v. Des Moines School District[69] as an act "closely akin" to speech or expression protected by the First Amendment. The unconstitutional school ban furthermore had little to do with "the requirements of appropriate discipline in the operation of the school."[70] It was found that the ban on armbands did not "concern aggressive, disruptive action or even group demonstrations . . . but only silent, passive expression of opinion. . . . In our system, undifferentiated fear or apprehension of disturbance is not enough to overcome the right to freedom of expression."[71]

The U.S. Supreme Court in McPherson v. Rankin[72] on June 24, 1978, ruled that a Texas county sheriff had violated the free speech rights of a clerical employee when he dismissed her for saying she hoped President Reagan would be assassinated. By a 5–4 vote, the Court affirmed her First Amendment rights to tell a coworker, after hearing a radio report on the attempted 1981 shooting of the president, that she hoped the next time the president would be fatally shot. The statement was not deemed to be a threat to kill the president, which would have been a crime unprotected by the First Amendment. Her "expression of hope" was symbolic speech, an expression of her opinion on a matter of "public concern"; defendant had criticized the president for hurting black people by cutting welfare programs. Accordingly, defendant could not be dismissed for impeding the efficiency of the sheriff's office since she had no law enforcement duties or any policy-making functions. Furthermore, her expression of opinion or hope took place where it could not be heard by members of the public, whose confidence in the sheriff's office could have been undermined. The concurring opinion by Justice Lewis Powell stated that the "unfortunate remark" to the coworker was "ill-considered, but protected. . . . If a statement is on a matter of public concern, as it was here, it will be an unusual case where the employer's legitimate interests will be so great as to justify punishing an employee for this type of private speech that routinely takes place at all levels of the workplace." Justice Marshall added: "Vigilance is necessary to insure that public employers do not use authority over employees to silence discourse, not because it hampers public functions but because superiors disagree with the content of employees' speech."[73]

2.5 TO PROTECT CHILDREN AND THE MENTALLY ILL

Over the entire range of speech or expression activities, courts have imposed paternalistic restraints on freedom of speech and of expression in order to advance health, education, and morals, particularly for children and the mentally ill.[74] For example, a child's freedom to peddle religious ideas may constitutionally be restricted to avoid "emotional excitement and psychological or physical injury."[75] A child's right of access to ideas, at least ideas that are vulgar or pornographic,[76] can be restricted on the ground that such matters impair the child's "ethical and moral development."[77] The mentally ill may constitutionally be limited, for example, by statutes authorizing censorship of incoming mail to promote the patient's welfare.[78] Even pencils, pens, or other writing paraphernalia may be taken from a mentally ill patient to prevent personal injury.[79]

The state has an interest as *parens patriae* in restricting freedom of speech and of expression, although it can be argued that paternalistic restrictions can be justified only on the assumption that the state is best able to choose on the individual's behalf and on behalf of society at large.[80] It is said that society has an interest in encouraging autonomy and diversity and that freedom of speech for children and even the mentally ill serves somewhat to advance those important interests.[81] To grant the child or the patient the greatest possible autonomy and diversity consistent with the purposes of child rearing or commitment, it is contended, is the *summum bonum*.

2.6 THE RIGHT TO PETITION GENERALLY

The right to petition the government for a redress of grievances is also subsumed under the First Amendment. Indeed, as the highest court observed in DeJonge v. Oregon,[82] a democratic government "implies a right on the part of its citizens to meet peaceably for consultation in respect to public affairs and to petition for redress of grievances." This fundamental right means simply that persons must have access to places where substantial numbers of persons congregate on a regular basis. In Lloyd v. Tanner,[83] the U.S. Supreme Court declared that handbilling by petitioners could be accomplished on public sidewalks surrounding a private shopping center where the handbills may be "distributed conveniently to pedestrians, and also to occupants of automobiles."

The U.S. Supreme Court in Martin v. Strothers[84] explained the rationale of this right to petition: "The right of freedom of speech and press has broad scope. The authors of the First Amendment knew that novel and unconventional ideas might disturb the complacent, but they chose to encourage a freedom which they believed essential if vigorous enlightenment was ever to triumph over slothful ignorance. This freedom embraces the right to distribute literature, and necessarily protects the right to receive it."[85] The highest court here invalidated a city ordinance that prohibited persons distributing handbills and circulars from ringing the doorbells or knocking on the doors of residences. And twenty-six years later in Red Lion Broadcasting Co. v. FCC,[86] the Court stated: "It is the purpose of the First Amendment to preserve an uninhibited marketplace of ideas in which truth will ultimately prevail. . . . It is the right of the public to receive suitable access to social, political, aesthetic, moral and other ideas and experiences which is crucial here. That right may not constitutionally be abridged."[87] The highest court, in Thomas v. Collins,[88] struck down a state statute requiring labor organizers to register with the state before soliciting union membership. In Lamont v. Postmaster General,[89] a federal act that allowed the postmaster general to detain "communist, political propaganda" in the mail was held unconstitutional as a "limitation on the unfettered exercise of the addressee's First Amendment rights."[90]

2.7 MISREPRESENTATION, DECEIT, OR FRAUD

The First Amendment to the U.S. Constitution proclaims that "Congress shall make no law . . . abridging the freedom of speech, or of the press." Therein lies a fundamental liberty of expression that cannot be abridged by the federal government or by state or local governments under the Fourteenth Amendment.[91] Freedom of speech means no restraints or limitations on misrepresentations, for example, whether the misrepresentation is commercial or noncommercial speech.[92]

Can government impose punitive damages or criminal fines and/or criminal penalties upon a person found "guilty" of committing the tort of misrepresentation, deceit, and fraud? Like freedom of speech or of expression, there is no absolute right. In times of war or similar crisis, the survival of the nation may be at stake, and reasonable restrictions are inevitable. Impugning the integrity of a court may place in jeopardy the administration of justice. Certainly public safety takes precedence over freedom of expression, and the states are bound thereby under the Fourteenth Amendment.[93] On the other hand, the U.S. Supreme Court in Cohen v. California[94] upset the conviction of a young man for wearing a shirt emblazoned with the words "Fuck the Draft": "The First and Fourteenth amendments must be taken to disable the States from punishing public utterance of this unseemly expletive in order to maintain what they regard as a suitable level of discourse within the body politic."

Part and parcel of freedom of expression is the right "to petition the government for a redress of grievances."[95] Petitioning may embrace misrepresentation, deceit, and fraud, and the right is fully protected, as voiced in 1972 by the U.S. Supreme Court in Lloyd v. Tanner,[96] which then declared that handbilling could be accomplished on public sidewalks surrounding a private shopping center because the handbills may be "distributed conveniently to pedestrians, and also to occupants of automobiles."

Defamation (libel and slander) is but one aspect of the misrepresentation tort, and it is in this context that First Amendment rights are often raised, as illustrated by Gertz v. Robert Welch, Inc.[97] Here, the U.S. Supreme Court held that punitive damages in libel actions contravened the guarantees of the First Amendment in cases in which the plaintiff failed to prove "constitutional malice" unless there was some fault on the part of the defendant. (Constitutional malice requires the speaker or publisher to be subjectively aware of the falsity of the defamatory representation.) Unless the speaker or publisher entertained serious doubts about the truth of the respresentation, punitive damages cannot be awarded. Thus, the states cannot impose liability without fault. In Wheeler v. Green,[98] the Oregon Supreme Court banned punitive damages based upon the freedom of press provision in the state constitution.

The U.S. Supreme Court in 1986 had occasion in Posadas de Puerto Rico Associates v. Tourism Company of Puerto Rico[99] to consider commercial free speech rights. A Puerto Rican statute and regulations restricted advertising of casino gambling aimed at residents, although it permitted advertising aimed at tourists. The Court first observed that commercial speech receives First Amendment protection so long as it concerns lawful activity and is not misleading or fraudulent. In a three-step analysis dictated by Central Hudson Gas & Electric Corp. v. Public Service Commission,[100] the Court ruled that the government's interest in restricting the speech was clearly "the reduction of demand for casino gambling by the residents of Puerto Rico. . . . Excessive casino gambling among local residents . . . would produce serious harmful effects on the health, safety, and welfare . . . such as the disruption of moral and cultural patterns, the increase in local crime, the fostering of prostitution, the development of corruption, and the infiltration of organized crime." Accordingly, the Puerto Rican statute did not violate the First Amendment; the statute and regulations thereunder were not unconstitutionally vague.

This elucidation of the First Amendment rights encompassed also in misrepresentation, deceit, and fraud can be pragmatically viewed by reference to the enforcement provisions of section 1983 of the U.S. Code, Title 42, which provides individuals with a private cause of action against any person who, under the color of state law, deprives the individual or individuals of rights guaranteed by federal law or the U.S. Constitution.[101] Section 1983, enacted in 1871, is one of the few avenues of judicial redress open to those seeking personal vindication of their constitutional rights. A plaintiff can sue state employees, local governments and their employees, as well as private parties, but the state itself under the Eleventh Amendment is given sovereign immunity from federal court judgments under section 1983.[102]

NOTES

1. 403 US 713 (1971).
2. Id. at pp. 726–27.
3. 444 US 507 (1980).
4. For lower court opinions, see 456 F Supp 176 (ED Va., 1978), modif 595 F2d 926 (4th Cir., 1979).
5. 94 Harv L Rev 1 (1980) at p. 9.
6. 435 US 765 (1978).
7. Id. at p. 783.
8. 435 US 829 (1978).
9. Id. at pp. 844–45.
10. See, for example, Erznoznik v. City of Jacksonville, 422 US 205 (1975).
11. 303 US 444 (1938).
12. 403 US 15 (1971).
13. Id. at p. 23.
14. 376 US 254 (1964).
15. Infra note 10 at p. 209.
16. 438 US 726 (1978).
17. 431 US 85 (1977).
18. 334 US 558 (1948).
19. See Breard v. Alexandria, 341 US 622 (1951).
20. 319 US 141 (1943).
21. Id. at p. 146.
22. Id. at p. 148. In City of New York v. American School Publications, Inc., 69 NY2d 972, 516 NYS2d 659 (1987) the highest New York court concluded that the First Amendment precluded the city of New York, in the absence of a local ordinance, from prohibiting the installation of sidewalk bins containing copies of defendant's publication. The city contended that the bins were "unsightly, unsanitary, and unsafe" and sued for an injunction restraining defendants from installing the bins. The city pointed out that the publication of the defendant was "commercial speech" and could be constitutionally prohibited from distribution in sidewalk bins. But the court ruled that the central issue was not whether or not the magazine constituted "commercial speech," but whether a government official may exercise "complete and unregulated discretion, in the absence of duly enacted guidelines or procedures, to decide which publications may be distributed via bins installed on city streets." For other decisions on the same point, see Plain Dealer Pub. Co. v. City of Lakewood, 794 F. 2d 1139 (6th Cir. 1986); Gannett Satellite Information Network, Inc. v. Metro Transp., 579 F. Supp. (SDNY 1984); Gannett Satellite Info. Network v. Town of Norwood, 579 F. Supp. 108 (D. Mass. 1984); Southern N.J. Newspapers v. State of N.J., etc., 542 F. Supp. 173 (D. N.J. 1982).
23. 680 P2d 666 (Ore App., 1986).
24. ORS Sec. 166.065(1)(b).
25. See Lewis v. Orleans, 415 US 130 (1974).
26. Id.
27. Id.
28. 303 US 444 (1938).
29. 345 US 402 (1950).

30. Id. at p. 409.
31. Id.
32. Id.
33. 104 S Ct 3262 (1984).
34. —NY2d—, —NE2d— (June 2, 1987).
35. See chapter 8 to this book.
36. Among the interesting cases cited by the court were Matter of Von Weigen, 63 NY2d 163, cert den sub nom Committee on Professonial Standards v.
Von Weigen, 105 S Ct 2701; Bolger v. Youngs Drug Products Corp., 463 US 60;
Central Hudson Gas & Electric Co. v. Public Service Commission, 447 US 539;
and Ohralik v. Ohio State Bar Assn, 436 US 447.
37. 55 USLW 4823 (1987).

The highest court found the Houston ordinance was substantially overbroad
since its literal wording punished and might deter a significant range of protected
speech. According to Justice Brennan,

The elements of First Amendment overbreadth analysis are familiar. Only a statute that is
substantially overbroad may be invalidated on its face. *New York* v. *Ferber*, 458 U.S. 747,
769 (1982); *Broadrick* v. *Oklahoma, supra.* "We have never held that a statute should be held
invalid on its face merely because it is possible to conceive of a single impermissible application. . . ." *Id.*, at 630 (BRENNAN, J., dissenting). Instead, "[i]n a facial challenge to the
overbreadth and vagueness of a law, a court's first task is to determine whether the enactment reaches a substantial amount of constitutionally protected conduct." *Hoffman Estates* v.
The Flipside, Hoffman Estates, Inc., 455 U.S. 489, 494 (1982); *Kolender* v. *Lawson*, 461 U.S.
352, 359, n. 8 (1983). Criminal statutes must be scrutinized with particular care, *e.g., Winters*
v. *New York*, 333 U.S. 507, 515 (1948); those that make unlawful a substantial amount of
constitutionally protected conduct may be held facially invalid even if they also have legitimate application. *E.g., Kolender, supra*, at 359, n. 8.

The City's principal argument is that the ordinance does not inhibit the exposition of ideas,
and that it bans "core criminal conduct" not protected by the First Amendment. Brief for
Appellant 12. In its view, the application of the ordinance to Hill illustrates that the police
employ it only to prohibit such conduct, and not "as a subterfuge to control or dissuade free
expression." *Ibid.* Since the ordinance is "content-neutral," and since there is no evidence
that the City has applied the ordinance to chill particular speakers or ideas, the City concludes that the ordinance is not substantially overbroad.

We disagree with the City's characterization for several reasons. First, the enforceable
portion of the ordinance deals not with core criminal conduct, but with speech. As the City
has conceded, the language in the ordinance making it unlawful for any person to "assault"
or "strike" a police officer is pre-empted by the Texas Penal Code. Reply Brief for Appellant
10. The City explains, *ibid.*, that "any species of physical assault on a police officer is encompassed within the provisions [§§22.01, 22.02] of the Texas Penal Code," and under §1.08 of
the Code, "[n]o governmental subdivision or agency may enact or enforce a law that makes
any conduct covered by this code an offense subject to a criminal penalty." Tex. Penal Code
Ann. §1.08 (1974). See *Knott* v. *State*, 648 S. W. 2d 20 (Tex. App. 1983) (reversing conviction obtained under municipal ordinance pre-empted by state penal code). Accordingly, the
enforceable portion of the ordinance makes it "unlawful for any person to . . . in any manner oppose, molest, abuse or interrupt any policeman in the execution of his duty," and
thereby prohibits verbal interruptions of police officers.

Second, contrary to the City's contention, the First Amendment protects a significant amount
of verbal criticism and challenge directed at police officers. "Speech is often provocative and
challenging. . . . [But it] is nevertheless protected against censorship or punishment, unless
shown likely to produce a clear and present danger of a serious substantive evil that rises far

above public inconvenience, annoyance, or unrest." *Terminiello* v. *Chicago*, 337 U.S. 1, 4 (1949). In *Lewis* v. *City of New Orleans*, 415 U.S. 130 (1974), for example, the appellant was found to have yelled obscenities and threats at an officer who had asked appellant's husband to produce his driver's license. Appellant was convicted under a municipal ordinance that made it a crime " 'for any person wantonly to curse or revile or to use obscene or opprobrious language toward or with reference to any member of the city police while in the actual performance of his duty.' " *Id.*, at 132 (citation omitted). We vacated the conviction and invalidated the ordinance as facially overbroad. Critical to our decision was the fact that the ordinance "punishe[d] only spoken words" and was not limited in scope to fighting words that " 'by their very utterance inflict injury or tend to incite an immediate breach of the peace.' " *Id.*, at 133, quoting *Gooding* v. *Wilson*, 405 U.S. 518, 525 (1972); see also *ibid.* (Georgia breach-of-peace statute not limited to fighting words held facially invalid). Moreover, in a concurring opinion in *Lewis*, JUSTICE POWELL suggested that even the "fighting words" exception recognized in *Chaplinsky* v. *New Hampshire*, 315 U.S. 568 (1942), might require a narrower application in cases involving words addressed to a police officer, because "a properly trained officer may reasonably be expected to 'exercise a higher degree of restraint' than the average citizen, and thus be less likely to respond belligerently to 'fighting words.' " 415 U.S., at 135 (citations omitted).

Justice Brennan concluded:

The Houston ordinance is much more sweeping than the municipal ordinance struck down in *Lewis*. It is not limited to fighting words nor even to obscene or opprobrious language, but prohibits speech that "in any manner . . . interrupt[s]" an officer. The Constitution does not allow such speech to be made a crime. The freedom of individuals verbally to oppose or challenge police action without thereby risking arrest is one of the principal characteristics by which we distinguish a free nation from a police state.

and

Houston's ordinance criminalizes a substantial amount of constitutionally protected speech, and accords the police unconstitutional discretion in enforcement. The ordinance's plain language is admittedly violated scores of times daily, App. 77, yet only some individuals—those chosen by the police in their unguided discretion—are arrested. Far from providing the "breathing space" that "First Amendment freedoms need . . . to survive," *NAACP* v. *Button*, 371 U.S. 415, 433 (1963), the ordinance is susceptible of regular application to protected expression. We conclude that the ordinance is substantially overbroad, and that the Court of Appeals did not err in holding it facially invalid. . . .

Today's decision reflects the constitutional requirement that, in the face of verbal challenges to police action, officers and municipalities must respond with restraint. We are mindful that the preservation of liberty depends in part upon the maintenance of social order. Cf. *Terminiello* v. *Chicago*, 337 U.S., at 37 (dissenting opinion). But the First Amendment recognizes, wisely we think, that a certain amount of expressive disorder not only is inevitable in a society committed to individual freedom, but must itself be protected if that freedom would survive.

The dissent of Justice Powell (joined in by Chief Justice Rehnquist, and by Justice Scalia in parts) emphasized that the

Court should not have reached the merits of the constitutional claims, but instead should have certified a question to the Texas Court of Criminal Appeals. I also disagree with the Court's reasons for declining to abstain under the principle of *Railroad Comm'n* v. *Pullman Co.*, 312 U.S. 496 (1941). Finally, although I agree that the ordinance as interpreted by the Court violates the Fourteenth Amendment, I write separately because I cannot join the

Court's reasoning. . . . I do agree that the ordinance can be applied to speech in some cases. And I also agree that the First Amendment protects a good deal of speech that may be directed at police officers. On occasion this may include verbal criticism, but I question the implication of the Court's opinion that the First Amendment generally protects verbal "challenge[s] directed at police officers," *ante*, at 9. A "challenge" often takes the form of opposition or interruption of performance of duty. In many situations, speech of this type directed at police officers will be functionally indistinguishable from conduct that the First Amendment clearly does not protect. For example, I have no doubt that a municipality constitutionally may punish an individual who chooses to stand near a police officer and persistently attempt to engage the officer in conversation while the officer is directing traffic at a busy intersection. Similarly, an individual, by contentious and abusive speech, could interrupt an officer's investigation of possible criminal conduct. A person observing an officer pursuing a person suspected of a felony could run beside him in a public street shouting at the officer. Similar tactics could interrupt a policeman lawfully attempting to interrogate persons believed to be witnesses to a crime.

In sum, the Court's opinion appears to reflect a failure to apprehend that this ordinance—however it may be construed—is intended primarily to further the public's interest in law enforcement. To be sure, there is a fine line between legitimate criticism of police and the type of criticism that interferes with the very purpose of having police officers. But the Court unfortunately seems to ignore this fine line and to extend First Amendment protection to any type of verbal molestation or interruption of an officer in the performance of his duty.

B

Despite the concerns expressed above, I nevertheless agree that the ambiguous terms of this ordinance "confe[r] on police a virtually unrestrained power to arrest and charge persons with a violation. . . . The opportunity for abuse, especially where a statute has received a virtually open-ended interpretation, is self-evident." *Lewis* v. *City of New Orleans, supra,* at 135–136 (POWELL, J., concurring in result). No Texas court has placed a limiting construction on the ordinance. Also, it is clear that Houston has made no effort to curtail the wide discretion of police officers under the present ordinance. . . . When government protects society's interests in a manner that restricts some speech the law must be framed more precisely than the ordinance before us. Accordingly, I agree with the Court that the Houston ordinance is unconstitutional.

It is difficult, of course, specifically to frame an ordinance that applies in

> "areas of human conduct where, by the nature of the problems presented, legislatures simply cannot establish standards with great precision. Control of the broad range of disorderly conduct that may inhibit a policeman in the peformance of his official duties may be one such area, requiring as it does an on-the-spot assessment of the need to keep order." *Smith* v. *Goguen*, 415 U.S. 566, 581 (1974).

In view of the difficulty of drafting precise language, that never restrains speech and yet serves the public interest, the attempts of States and municipalities to draft laws of this type should be accorded some leeway. I am convinced, however, that the Houston ordinance is too vague to comport with the First and Fourteenth Amendments. As I explained *supra*, at 2, it should be possible for the present ordinance to be reframed in a way that would limit the present broad discretion of officers and at the same time protect substantially the city's legitimate interests. For example, the ordinance could make clear that it applies to speech only if the purpose of the speech were to interfere with the performance by a police officer of his lawful duties. In this situation, the difficulties of drafting precisely should not justify upholding this ordinance.

38.   —F Supp— (SDNY, 1987). The U.S. Supreme Court in Board of Airport Commissioners of the City of Los Angeles v. Jews for Jesus, Inc., 55 USLW 4855

(1987) found a Los Angeles resolution banning all "First Amendment activities" within the international airport to violated the First Amendment because the airport was a traditional public forum under federal law. Justice O'Connor pointed out that

> In balancing the government's interest in limiting the use of its property against the interests of those who wish to use the property for expressive activity, the Court has identified three types of fora: the traditional public forum, the public forum created by government designation, and the nonpublic forum. *Perry Ed. Assn.* v. *Perry Local Educators' Assn.*, 460 U.S. 37, 45–46 (1983). The proper First Amendment analysis differs depending on whether the area in question falls in one category rather than another. In a traditional public forum or a public forum by government designation, we have held that First Amendment protections are subject to heightened scrutiny:
>> "In these quintessential public forums, the government may not prohibit all communicative activity. For the State to enforce a content-based exclusion it must show that its regulation is necessary to serve a compelling state interest and that it is narrowly drawn to achieve that end. . . . The State may also enforce regulations of the time, place, and manner of expression which are content-neutral, are narrowly tailored to serve a significant government interest, and leave open ample alternative channels of communication." *Id.* at 45.
> We have further held, however, that access to a nonpublic forum may be restricted by government regulation as long as the regulation "is reasonable and not an effort to suppress expression merely because officials oppose the speaker's view." *Id.*, at 46.
> The petitioners content that LAX is neither a traditional public forum nor a public forum by government designation, and accordingly argue that the latter standard governing access to a nonpublic forum is appropriate. The respondents, in turn, argue that LAX is a public forum subject only to reasonable time, place or manner restrictions. . . .
> Under the First Amendment overbreadth doctrine, an individual whose own speech or conduct may be prohibited is permitted to challenge a statute on its face "because it also threatens others not before the court—those who desire to engage in legally protected expression but who may refrain from doing so rather than risk prosecution or undertake to have the law declared partially invalid." *Brockett* v. *Spokane Arcades, Inc.*, 472 U.S. 491, 503 (1985). A statute may be invalidated on its face, however, only if the overbreadth is "substantial." *Houston* v. *Hill*,—U.S.—, —(1987); *New York* v. *Ferber*, 458 U.S. 747, 769 (1982); *Broadrick* v. *Oklahoma*, 413 U.S. 601, 615 (1973). The requirement that the overbreadth be substantial arose from our recognition that application of the overbreadth doctrine is, "manifestly, strong medicine," *Broadrick* v. *Oklahoma, supra,* at 613, and that "there must be a realistic danger that the statute itself will significantly compromise recognized First Amendment protections of parties not before the Court for it to be facially challenged on overbreadth grounds." *City Council* v. *Taxpayers for Vincent*, 466 U.S. 789, 801 (1984).
> On its face, the resolution at issue in this case reaches the universe of expressive activity, and, by prohibiting *all* protected expression, purports to create a virtual "First Amendment Free Zone" at LAX. The resolution does not merely regulate expressive activity in the Central Terminal Area that might create problems such as congestion or the disruption of the activities of those who use LAX. Instead, the resolution expansively states that LAX "is not open for First Amendment activities by any individual and/or entity," and that "any individual and/or entity [who] seeks to engage in First Amendment activities within the Central Terminal Area . . . shall be deemed to be acting in contravention of the stated policy of the Board of Airport Commissioners." App. 4a–5a. The resolution therefore does not merely reach the activity of respondents at LAX; it prohibits even talking and reading, or the wearing of campaign buttons or symbolic clothing. Under such a sweeping ban, virtually every

individual who enters LAX may be found to violate the resolution by engaging in some "First Amendment activit[y]." We think it is obvious that such a ban cannot be justified even if LAX were a nonpublic forum because no conceivable governmental interest would justify such an absolute prohibition of speech.

The petitioners suggest that the resolution is not substantially overbroad because it is intended to reach only expressive activity unrelated to airport-related purposes. Such a limiting construction, however, is of little assistance in substantially reducing the overbreadth of the resolution. Much nondisruptive speech—such as the wearing of a T-Shirt or button that contains a political message—may not be "airport related," but is still protected speech even in a nonpublic forum. See *Cohen* v. *California*, 403 U.S. 15 (1971). Moreover, the vagueness of this suggested construction itself presents serious constitutional difficulty. The line between airport-related speech and nonairport-related speech is, at best, murky. The petitioners, for example, suggest that an individual who reads a newspaper or converses with a neighbor at LAX is engaged in permitted "airport-related" activity because reading or conversing permits the traveling public to "pass the time." Reply Brief for Petitioners 12. We presume, however, that petitioners would not so categorize the activities of a member of a religious or political organization who decides to "pass the time" by distributing leaflets to fellow travelers. In essence, the result of this vague limiting construction would be to give LAX officials alone the power to decide in the first instance whether a given activity is airport related. Such a law that "confers on police a virtually unrestrained power to arrest and charge persons with a violation" of the resolution is unconstitutional because "[t]he opportunity for abuse, especially where a statute has received a virtually open-ended interpretation, is self-evident." *Lewis* v. *City of New Orleans*, 415 U.S. 130, 135–136 (1974) (POWELL, J., concurring); see also *Houston* v. *Hill*, —U.S., at—; *Kolender* v. *Lawson*, 461 U.S. 352, 358 (1983).

We conclude that the resolution is substantially overbroad, and is not fairly subject to a limiting construction. Accordingly, we hold that the resolution violates the First Amendment.

39. Beverly Oil Co. v. City of Los Angeles, 254 P2d 865 (Cal., 1953).

40. See 10 Golden Gate U L Rev 805 (1980) at p. 834.

41. See Alderwood Associates v. Washington Environmental Council, 635 P2d 108 (Wash., 1981), Stafford, Justice dissenting at p. 121.

42. 592 P2d 341 (Cal., 1979).

43. The California court cited A.L.R.B. v. Superior Court, 546 P2d 687 (Cal., 1976), for the proposition that "all private property is held subject to the power of government to regulate its use for the public welfare."

44. Infra note 41 at p. 346.

45. 452 US 640 (1981).

46. Note that the Court was concerned that any exemption applied to the Krishna Society would have to apply equally to a large number of other groups, such as religious, social, political, charitable, and perhaps even commercial organizations. The Krishna Society did not have any "special claim to First Amendment protection as compared to that of other religions who also distribute literature and who also solicit funds." Infra note 43 at p. 652.

47. 452 US 76 (1981).

48. 453 US 490 (1981).

49. See section 8.1 herein.

50. 620 SW2d 833 (Tex. Civ App., 1981).

51. 620 generally 13 Tech Tech L Rev 1512 (1982).

52. Infra note 47 at p. 836.

53. See section 2.2 above.

54. Infra note 49 at p. 837.
55. 615 SW2d 202 (Tex., 1981).
56. See Gannett Co. v. City of Rochester, 330 NYS2d 648 (1972).
57. See Martin v. City of Struthers, 319 US 141 (1943).
58. See Flower v. United States, 407 US 197 (1972).
59. See Hague v. Congress of Industrial Organizations, 307 US 496 (1939). Note the statement of Justice Roberts in Schneider v. State, 308 US 147 (1939):

Municipal authorities, as trustees for the public, have the duty to keep their communities' streets open and available for movement of people and property, the primary purpose to which the streets are dedicated. So long as legislation to this end does not abridge the constitutional liberty of one rightfully upon the street to impart information through speech or the distribution of literature, it may lawfully regulate the conduct of those using the streets. For example, a person could not exercise this liberty by taking his stand in the middle of a crowded street, contrary to traffic regulations, and maintain his position to the stoppage of all traffic; a group of distributors could not insist upon a constitutional right to form a cordon across the street and to allow no pedestrian to pass who did not accept a tendered leaflet. . . . Prohibition of such a conduct would not abridge the constitutional liberty since such activity bears no necessary relationship to the freedom to speak, write, print or distribute information or opinion. (Pp. 160–61)

Note that the New York court in Town of Islip v. Caviglia, —NYS2d—(August 11, 1987) upheld that adult business provisions of the Islip Town Code as valid and enforceable, despite the fact that adult bookstore had to be removed. According to the court,

the Town has not used this power (of zoning) to zone as a pretext for suppressing expression, but rather has sought to make some areas available for adult business and their patrons while at the same time preserving the quality of life in the community at large by preventing those businesses from locating in other areas. . . . The ordinance by its terms is designated to prevent crime, protect the Town's retail trade, maintain property values, and generally protect and preserve the quality of life in the Town and not to suppress the expression of unpopular views.

(The court cited City of Renton v. Playtime Theatres, Inc. 106 S Ct 925 (1986):

There is no constitutional deficit in the method chosen by the town to further its substantial interest. A municipality may regulate adult businesses by dispersing them or by concentrating them (City of Renton v. Playtime Theatres, Inc., supra).

In concentrating adult businesses in Industrial Districts, the town sought to lessen the impact these businesses have on the business and residential districts. The industrial Districts consist of some 6,000 acres of land with over eighty six miles of frontage on open roadways where adult businesses may be established. Thus, there is ample accessible real estate available for those businesses and the Town has met the requirement that reasonable alternative avenues of communication be provided.

60. Infra note 44.
61. Also see Cox v. New Hampshire, 311 US 451 (1941):

The authority of a municipality to impose regulations in order to assure the safety and convenience of the people in the use of public highways has never been regarded as inconsistent with civil liberties but rather as one of the means of safeguarding the good order upon which they ultimately depend. The control of travel on the streets of cities is the most familiar illustration of this recognition of social need. Where a restriction of the use of highways in that relation is designed to promote the public convenience in the interest of all, it cannot be disregarded by the attempted exercise of some civil right which in other circumstances would be entitled to protection. One would not be justified in ignoring the familiar red traffic light because he thought it his religious duty to disobey the municipal command or sought by that means to direct public attention to an announcement of his opinions.

62. 283 US 359 (1931).
63. See section 8.2 herein.
64. 319 US 624 (1943).
65. Id. at p. 642.
66. 391 US 367 (1968).
67. Id. at p. 376.
68. Id. at p. 377.
69. 393 US 505 (1969).
70. Id. at p. 509.
71. Id.
72. 55 USLW 5019 (1987); lower court at 786 F2d 1233 (5th Cir., 1986).
73. Id. Also see New York Times (June 25, 1987) at p. B13.
74. See generally 94 Harv L Rev 1756 (1981) at pp. 1768 et seq.
75. See Prince v. Massachusetts, 321 US 158 (1944) at p. 170. Also see Eisenstadt v. Baird, 405 US 438 (1972) at pp. 443–46.
Note City of Newport v. Iacobucci, 107 S Ct 383 (1987) where the U.S. Supreme Court sanctioned a State's power to regulate the sale of liquor under the Twenty-First Amendment by a city ordinance prohibiting, in places that sell alcohol for drinking on the premises, nude or nearly-nude dancing that otherwise might be protected under the First Amendment. (The decision was 5–2.)
76. See chapter 10 to this book.
77. See Ginsberg v. New York, 390 US 629 (1968).
78. See S.C. Code, Sec. 44–23–1030(1); also note Wyatt v. Aderholt, 503 F2d 1305 (5th Cir., 1974).
79. See Minn Stat Sec. 253A.17.4 (1980).
80. Infra note 73 at p. 1771.
81. See Meyer v. Nebraska, 262 US 390 (1923) at pp. 401–2.
82. 299 US 353 (1937) at p. 364.
83. 407 US 551 (1972).
84. 319 US 141 (1943); see also 4 U Haw L Rev (1982) at p. 130.
85. Id. at p. 143.
86. 395 US 367 (1969).
87. Id. at pp. 389–90.
88. 323 US 516 (1945).
89. 381 US 301 (1965).
90. Id. at p. 305.
91. See chapters 1, 3, and 4 hereinbefore.
92. Note United States v. Progressive, Inc., 467 F Supp 990 (WD Wisc., 1979), app dism 610 F2d 819 (7th Cir., 1979).
93. See Hall v. May Department Stores Co., 292 Ore 131, 637 P2d 126 (1981).
94. 403 US 15 (1971).
95. According to the First Amendment, as quoted.
96. 407 US 551 (1972).

97. 418 US 323 (1974).
98. 593 P2d 777 (Ore., 1977).
99. 106 S Ct 2968 (1986).
100. 447 US 557 (1980).
101. 42 USC 1983 (1982) read as follows:

Every person who, under color of any statute, ordinance, regulation, custom, or usage of any State or Territory or the District of Columbia, subjects, or causes to be subjected, any citizen of the United States or other person within the jurisdiction thereof, to the deprivation of any rights, privileges, or immunities secured by the Constitution and laws, shall be liable to the party injured in an action at law, suit in equity, or other proper proceeding for redress.

102. See Quern v. Jordan, 440 US 332 (1979).

3

Private Property and the Right to a Forum for Expression

The First Amendment admittedly does not preclude private abridgment of freedom of speech, for the ban is against government—federal, state, and local. Yet private property has supplanted public property as the base for much community activity, and so freedom of speech may be abridged when access is denied to private property as a forum for expression. The relationship between the rights of private property ownership and the exercise of First Amendment rights has been the subject of much litigation over the years.[1] Since private property rights and speech rights exist in tension, the elevation of one over the other in a given situation is necessarily at the expense of the other.

It was in 1946 that the U.S. Supreme Court first decided, in Marsh v. Alabama,[2] that a privately owned company town was the "functional equivalent" of the public business district. Since that time, socioeconomic changes have altered the nature and size of shopping centers and shopping malls, as well as corporate business complexes, which have supplanted the public parks, public streets, and public areas as the sites where people congregate. They are today the popular forums for expression under the First Amendment.

Before the twentieth century, as exemplified in 1897 by Davis v. Massachusetts,[3] the state legislature was considered to be the owner of public streets and public parks belonging to the state and therefore had the owner's absolute control over public speaking on public streets and public parks. That view was subsequently replaced by such decisions as Jamison v. Texas,[4] which held that public speaking, including such speech-related activities as parading on public streets, public sidewalks, and in public parks, could neither be banned nor subjected to discretionary licensing. In Southeastern Promotions, Ltd. v. Conrad,[5] a privately owned theater leased to the municipality was deemed to be a public forum "designed for and dedicated to expressive activities"; thus, refusal to permit the showing of the musical *Hair* constituted a prior restraint forbidden under the First Amendment. Government today cannot regulate speech-related activities in public forums except in very narrow ways proved to serve significant governmental interests. Such activities in public forums cannot be put off-limits merely to save public expense or minimize public inconvenience.

The Michigan Supreme Court in 1963, in Amalgamated Clothing Workers v. Wonderland Shopping Center,[6] enjoined interference with the union's distribution of handbills (urging people not to buy nonunion shirts) on the exterior sidewalk of a shopping center, which the court labeled "quasi-public in nature," although it was privately owned. To justify the conclusion that the shopping center in 1963 should be treated as "public property" for purposes of the First Amendment as well as the free speech provision of the Michigan Constitution, the court opined:

Private property may, by unceremonious act and implication from an act on part of the landowner, and like act and implication from act on the part of the public, become subject to public easement by means of common law dedication. The public right in such instance does not depend upon acceptance and use for any particular period of years. The fact of dedication and acceptance, and the extent of the dedicated use, must be determined from the intent of the dedicators and acceptors and the legal significations thereof. No particular form is necessary to such dedication. The fee does not pass. An easement does. There may be a public abandonment after acceptance, and reversion to the original owner, when the use for which the dedication was made becomes impossible of execution or where the object of the use fails. . . . The change from the operation of a single store by a storekeeper to a large, complex, multiple shopping center, alters the very nature of the operation from one of purely private character to one of public or quasi-public character. . . . The property of the defendants has lost its identity as private property."[7]

In the 1946 ruling in Marsh v. Alabama,[8] Justice Hugo Black wrote that "the more an owner, for his advantage, opens up his property for use by the public in general, the more do his rights become circumscribed by the statutory and constitutional rights of those who use it."[9] The similarities between the company town in 1946 and a shopping center in 1968 prompted the highest court to conclude in Food Employees Union v. Logan Valley Plaza, Inc.[10] that they were "functionally equivalent," thereby giving the labor union protection of its First Amendment rights.[11] The contrary view appeared in the 1976 decision of the U.S. Supreme Court in Hudgens v. National Labor Relations Board:[12] "The property of a large shopping center is 'open to the public,' serves the same purpose as a 'business district' of a municipality and therefore has been dedicated to certain types of public use. The constitution by no means requires such an attenuated doctrine of dedication of private property to public use."[13] In essence, the Hudgens case decided that reasonable restraints imposed by a privately owned shopping center was not governmental action and therefore was not constitutionally prohibited. But four years later, in 1980, in Robins v. Pruneyard Shopping Center,[14] the highest court found that the free speech and freedom to petition provisions of the California Constitution protected a right of access in the common areas of a privately owned shopping mall. These fundamental rights "justified reasonable restrictions on private property rights." The property owners of the Pruneyard Shopping Center (who sought to bar a group of high school students from soliciting signatures in support of a petition protesting a United Nations resolution equating zionism with racism) contended that their property rights were infringed under the First, Fifth, and Fourteenth amendments. The Court rejected these arguments, pointing out that there was no evidence that the First Amendment activity interfered with the mall's normal business operations; furthermore, since the mall "by choice of its owner" was not limited to personal use but was open to the public, the expressed views of the public are entitled to protection. The dissent of Justice Marshall in Hudgens[15] sums up the picture: "The owner of the modern shopping center complex . . . to some extent displaces the 'State' from control of historical First Amendment forums."[16]

The California court in the Pruneyard Shopping Center case[17] relied to a great extent on the inherent state police power to regulate property for legitimate purposes.[18] There was a state interest in strengthening First Amendment rights, and the state court balanced that interest against the asserted property interests of the owners of the shopping center whose property was freely accessible to the public. The court concluded that property may be regulated by requiring shopping center owners to permit reasonably exercised speech and petitioning activity on their premises. Incidentally, there would be no constitutional difficulty if one state imposed more rigorous regulation on property rights than another state, as long as the supremacy of federal law is recognized[19] and the state interpretation does not impinge on a countervailing federal right.[20]

Private property is said to reflect the social fabric of society, and the absoluteness of ownership has long been modified to serve the collective needs of society at large. One example is found in Spence v. Washington,[21] where the Washington Supreme Court opined that the defendant could not in violation of a Washington statute "place any design upon any flag," thereby jeopardizing his freedom of expression. The state's interest in preserving the symbolic integrity of the American flag was sufficiently important to curb defendant's use of his privately owned flag—his private property right—so that he could not convey other messages. But the U.S. Supreme Court reversed the conviction because it found no permanent injury to the flag by defendant's act of displaying it upside down and attaching a peace symbol to it. The First Amendment triumphed (together with defendant's property rights) in the same decision.[22]

The next year, in Southeastern Promotions, Ltd. v. Conrad,[23] the highest court established a right to a public forum when it found that the city had violated the First Amendment rights of the producers of the rock musical *Hair* in refusing to allow a performance of it in the municipal theater. The Washington Supreme Court in its 1981 decision in Alderwood Associates v. Washington Environmental Council[24] summarily dismissed the mall owner's private autonomy interests as "quite minimal in the context of shopping centers" and protected the First Amendment rights of those soliciting signatures in the shopping center. The dissent of Justice Marshall in Lloyd Corp. v. Tanner[25] summed it up: "We must remember that it is a balance that we are striking—a balance between freedom to speak, a freedom that is given a preferred place in our hierarchy of values, and the freedom of a private property owner to control his property. When the competing interests are fairly weighed, the balance can only be struck in favor of speech." Eight years later, the U.S. Supreme Court in the Pruneyard Shopping Center case reiterated that property owners may not use their property to "the detriment of society." At the same time, the New Jersey Supreme Court in State v. Schmid[26] found that Princeton University had violated the petitioner's constitutional rights of speech and of assembly when the university had petitioner arrested for distributing political materials on campus. The Connecticut Supreme Court in Cologne v. Westfarms Associates[27] observed that there was no legal basis to distinguish shopping malls, for example, from other places where large numbers of people congregate (thereby perhaps affording superior accommodations for political activities), such as sports stadiums, convention halls, theaters, and even university campuses. But that court, in a 3–2 decisison, held that the free speech and petition provisions of the Connecticut Constitution are not applicable to private shopping centers. The Michigan Supreme Court in Woodland v. Michigan Citizens Lobby[28] similarly ruled that the state constitution did not prevent owners of large shopping malls from denying or restricting access to private individuals seeking to exercise First Amendment rights: "The Michigan Constitution's Declaration of Rights provisions have never been interpreted as extending to purely private conduct; these provisions have consistently been interpreted as limited to protection against State action."[29]

It should be clear that public facilities created for the primary purpose of public communication are ideal forums under the First Amendment. What triggers the public forum is its deliberate use as a place for the exchange of views among members of the public. Public schools and public libraries, which admittedly have other public purposes, are not created for public exchange so the government can properly regulate to preserve the decorum of the classroom and the tranquility of the library.[30] Government may exclude even peaceful speech that interferes, instrumentally or symbolically, with the function of government institutions. It may not, however, exclude peaceful speech compatible with the purposes of the public schools or libraries. For example, in Kiiskila v. Nichols,[31] the plaintiff, a civilian worker on a military base, was fired because she passed out antiwar literature near (but not on) the military base. The federal district appellate court ruled in her favor under the First Amendment. But in Greer v. Spock,[32] the U.S. Supreme Court invalidated a lower court injunction that had compelled Fort Dix to allow presidential candidate Dr. Benjamin Spock and his followers to speak on the military base. The Court tersely stated that the primary purpose of military bases is "to train soldiers, not to provide a public forum."[33] A municipal transit system was the situs for a municipal policy permitting paid commercial advertising but not paid political advertising in Lehman v. City of Shaker Heights.[34] The highest court upheld the constitutionality of the municipal policy by categorizing the city transit system as the site of a commercial venture and not a public forum; furthermore, the city of Shaker Heights was interested in maximizing revenues to be earned from long-time commercial advertising as opposed to ephemeral political advertising.[35] Justice William O. Douglas in a separate opinion opined that commuters on the city's transit system had a right not to be accosted by political advertisements. But it was this very discrimination between commercial speech and political speech that was at the core of the four dissenting opinions.

Public hospitals do not provide a base for freedom of speech activity, as solemnized in Pickens v. State of Texas,[36] where a parolee had his parole rescinded based upon his exercise of free speech that was not permitted under the circumstances of the place, time, and manner. Public universities are not the sites for "political speech," as shown in Healy v. James,[37] where the Court ruled in favor of the students but cautioned that political speech on college campuses may be curtailed whenever it is likely to "materially and substantially disrupt the work and discipline of the school."[38] The Fourth U.S. Court of Appeals in Thonen v. Jenkins[39] ordered the reinstatement of a group of students who had been suspended for writing a letter to the editor of the university newspaper in which the college president was described in "obscene terms."[40] Freedom of speech prevailed over property rights because of the clear government commitment, as exemplified in Associated Press v. United States,[41] "to the widest possible dissemination of information".

But private property interests, as elaborated on in Amalgamated Clothing Workers v. Wonderland Shopping Centers,[42] place the home owner's right to exclude unwanted views above the speaker's desire to intrude them.

In a similar vein is the residential letter box or private mailbox, which the U.S. Supreme Court delineated in its 1981 decision of United States Postal Service v. Council of Greenburgh Civil Associations.[43] The Court ruled that a residential letter box or private mailbox did not constitute a "public forum" to which the First Amendment guarantees access to all persons.[44] The Court upheld the Postal Service's prohibition on the deposit of nonpostage material into these residential letter boxes or private mailboxes. The dissenting opinion of Justice Marshall stressed the inequity of the prohibition: "By traveling door to door to hand-deliver their messages to the homes of community members, appellees employ the method of written expression most accessible to those who are not powerful, established, or well-financed."[45] But the public forum concept precluding restraints upon freedom of expression still excludes public forum status to jails,[46] to transit lines,[47] and to military bases,[48] for example. However, the public forum is subject to reasonable time, place, and manner restrictions,[49] as illustrated by Grayned v. City of Rockford,[50] where the U.S. Supreme Court in 1972 upheld a municipal ordinance prohibiting any action on or near public school property while classes were in session. Grayned was arrested while participating in a racially motivated public demonstration on a sidewalk adjacent to the public school grounds. Justice Marshall, while agreeing that sidewalks are traditional public forums, nevertheless pointed out: "Noisy demonstrations that disrupt or are incompatible with normal school activities are obviously within the ordinance's reach. . . . The crucial question is whether the manner of expression is basically incompatible with the normal activity of a particular place at a particular time."[51]

The U.S. Supreme Court on June 15, 1987, in Board of Airport Commissioners v. Jews for Jesus[52] reviewed an ordinance of the city of Los Angeles that barred First Amendment activities within the central terminal of the Los Angeles International Airport. In 1984, a member of a group calling themselves Jews for Jesus was stopped by a police officer while distributing leaflets at the airport. The federal district court found that the airport was a public forum, and there were no compelling reasons to justify a total ban on such First Amendment activities. The Ninth U.S. Court of Appeals affirmed, and Justice Sandra Day O'Connor, writing for the court, agreed, pointing out that the ordinance was so broad it "prohibits even talking and reading, or the wearing of campaign buttons or symbolic clothing." But Justice O'Connor stated that it was not necessary to decide whether airports are public forums because "such a ban cannot be justified even if LAX [the airport] were a non-public forum because no conceivable governmental interest would justify such an absolute prohibition of speech. . . . Virtually every individual who enters the airport may be found to violate the resolution."

Professor Tucker in his 1985 book, *Law, Liberalism and Free Speech*, took occasion to enunciate the following pertinent principles:

(a) No owner (not even a governmental authority) is obliged to make a resource available for use as a forum. Governments do, of course, have a general obligation to ensure that a sufficient number of forums are available, and streets and parks have usually been put to such a use. This general obligation does not fall upon every government agency, however, and in some circumstances there may be good reasons for not making a forum available for public use. (Thus, if a government-funded broadcasting station or transit authority refused to carry advertising, they would be clearly entitled to take this stand.) (b) Functionally relevant regulations may be imposed. Finally, (c) discriminations which are content-specific should not be imposed. Thus, a broadcaster who sells advertising spots ought not to control the messages carried and—apart from setting functionally relevant administrative standards, allowed for under (b)—must accept the advertising of all who are willing to pay for it on an equal basis.

Perhaps the most serious challenge to these principles calls (c) into question, for it has been held (by no less an authority than the United States Supreme Court) that discriminations which are not content-neutral may, nevertheless, be functionally relevant to the purposes for which a forum is used, and are sometimes tolerable as an insignificant abridgment of the right to communicate under principle (b).[53]

Professor Tucker observed that "the occasion for this judgment" concerned the case of Lehman v. City of Shaker Heights,[54] wherein the defendant city refused to carry a politician's political advertisements in municipal buses, and the U.S. Supreme Court upheld the city, for such advertising "does not rise to the dignity of a First Amendment violation."[55] The author concluded that "bus cards are not a very significant forum, and it is not surprising that no great fuss was made when political advertisers were excluded from obtaining access to the buses. . . ."[56]

NOTES

1. See generally Tribe, American Constitutional Law (1978) at sec. 12–21.
2. 326 US 501 (1946).
3. 167 US 43 (1897) at pp. 47–48.
4. 318 US 413 (1943).
5. 420 US 546 (1976).
6. 122 NW2d 785 (Mich., 1963).
7. Id. Cf. Woodland v. Michigan Citizens Lobby, 378 NW2d 337 (Mich., 1985).
8. Infra note 2.
9. Id. at p. 506.
10. Infra note 20.
11. See generally 18 Gonzaga L Rev 81 (1982–1983) at p. 88.
12. 424 US 507 (1976).
13. Id. at p. 519.
14. 100 S Ct 2035 (1980).
15. Infra note 12.
16. Id. at p. 539.

17. Infra note 56; also 592 P2d 341 (Cal., 1979).

18. See section 2.2.

Note People v. Holman, 68 NY2d 202 (October 21, 1987) where New York's highest court upheld defendant's convictions for unlawful exposure as a result of his nude bathing on a public beach:

"it cannot be said that nude sunbathing is a form of expression likely to be understood by the viewer as an attempt to convey a particular point of view," hence, the activity has not a fundamental right entitled to First Amendment protection."

19. Note Article 3, section 1, of the California Constitution, which reads: "The State of California is an inseparable part of the United States of America, and the United States Constitution is the supreme law of the land."

20. The U.S. Supreme Court has consistently held that the states are free to adopt higher standards, as seen in Cooper v. California, 386 US 58 (1967), Oregon v. Hass, 420 US 714 (1975), and Johnson v. New Jersey, 384 US 719 (1966).

21. 418 US 405 (1974).

22. See 94 Harv L Rev 1 (1980) at pp. 49–50.

23. 420 US 546 (1975), infra note 5.

24. 635 P2d 108 (Wash., 1981).

25. 407 US 551 (1972) at pp. 580 et seq.

26. 85 NJ 535, 423 A2d 615 (1980), app dism 102 S Ct 867 (1982).

27. 469 A2d 1201 (Conn., 1984).

28. 378 NW2d 337 (Mich., 1985).

29. The Michigan court continued:

The history of Michigan's Constitutional Convention supports the proposition that, generally, the reach of individual rights afforded by the Michigan Constitution is limited to protection against government. . . .

The State action limitation is supported and reinforced by the separation of powers doctrine because of the recognition that the courts are inherently limited, because of their institutional character and role, to accomplish goals which are essentially legislative and political. This element of the State action requirement is supported by logic and practical considerations as well. . . . It may not be presumed that the constitutional provisions here in question are intended to apply against private individuals or entities. If any presumption is to be raised, it is to the contrary: that unless otherwise expressed, constitutionally guaranteed protections are applicable only against government. . . . If the citizens of Michigan wish their constitution in addition to serving as a shield against the actions of the State, to be used as a sword by individuals against individuals, there is a means by which this can be done.

30. See Grayned v. City of Rockford, 408 US 104 (1972).

31. 433 F2d 745 (7th Cir., 1970).

32. 424 US 828 (1976).

33. Id. at p. 828.

34. 418 US 298 (1974).

35. See section 8.2 herein.

36. 497 F2d 981 (1974), cert den 419 US 880 (1974).

37. 408 US 169 (1972).

38. Id. at p. 189.

39. 491 F2d 722 (4th Cir., 1973).

40. Id. at p. 723.

41. 326 US 1 (1945).
42. Infra note 6.
43. 101 S Ct 2676 (1981); also see 21 Washburn L J (1984).
44. See generally 26 UCLA L Rev 1410 (1979).
45. Infra note 43 at p. 2692.
46. See Adderly v. Florida, 385 US 39 (1966).
47. See Lehman v. City of Shaker Heights, 418 US 298 (1974).
48. See Greer v. Spock, 424 US 828 (1976).
49. Infra note 43 at p. 414.
50. 408 US 104 (1972).
51. Infra note 50 at p. 120.
52. 55 USLW 4855 (1987), affd 785 F2d 791 (9th Cir., 1986).
53. At p. 69–70.
54. Infra note 34.
55.

Lehman was standing as a candidate in an election for the State Assembly, argued that because the transit authority already carried commercial and public service advertising its rejection of his material was discriminatory. Of course, if the authority's buses already carried political advertising, the case would have been perfectly straightforward. However, it had rejected all advertising of a political nature and not just Lehman's posters, treating all the contesting candidates in a similar way.

In his judgment for the majority, Justice Blackmun concedes that "the policies and practices governing access to the transit system's advertising space must not be arbitrary, capricious or invidious." However, he goes on to argue that the managerial decision to limit the car card space to commercial and service-oriented advertising "does not rise to the dignity of a First Amendment violation" of this kind. According to Blackmun, administrative interests informed the managerial decision to discriminate against those who wish to convey political messages. He tells us,

> Revenue earned from long-term commercial advertising could be jeopardized by a requirement that short-term candidacy or issue-orientated advertisements be displayed on car cards. Users would be subjected to the blare of political propaganda. There could be lurking doubts about favoritism, and sticky administrative problems might arise in parceling out limited space to eager politicians.

And he goes on to claim, "These are reasonable legislative objectives advanced by the city in a proprietary capacity."

Bus cards are not a very significant forum, and perhaps an issue of such trivial dimensions should not be considered worthy of principled and considered adjudication. But what if every advertising forum were closed to political advertisers? A possibility which Blackmun's judgment does not exclude is that radio stations and television companies may well decide (because political campaigns are a nuisance and entail extra administrative burdens) to give commercial advertisers preference. This is a problem with the *Lehman v. City of Shaker Heights* judgment for, in recognizing someone's claim to a discretionary power, it is not a good practice to assume that he is going to use it in a particular way. We need to find a principled basis for deciding whether he should be afforded the authority claimed. In this regard, Blackmun's reasoning not only calls my principle of content neutrality into question but departs from the approach developed by the United States Supreme Court in previous public forum cases, where the tendency has been to insist that administrative discretions be very narrowly defined.

Infra note 53 at pp. 70–71.
56. Id. at p. 71.

4

State Action Under the First and Fourteenth Amendments

The "State action" doctrine, delineated herein, has long established that, due to language or history, most provisions of the Constitution and Amendments thereto, protecting individual liberty, impose important restrictions or obligations only upon government, both state and federal. The Civil Rights Cases[1] in 1883—holding that neither the Thirteenth nor the Fourteenth Amendments empowered Congress to pass the Civil Rights Act of 1875 making unlawful racial discrimination in public accommodations like inns or hotels, public conveyances or public places of amusement—gave some truth to the concept of "State action." The highest court here opined that under the Fourteenth Amendment

it is the State action of a particular character that is prohibited. Individual invasion of individual rights is not the subject-matter of the Amendment. . . . It nullifies and makes void all state legislation, and state action of every kind, which impairs the privileges and immunities of citizens of the United States, or which injures them in life, liberty, or property without due process of law, or which denies to any of them the equal protection of the laws. [T]he last section of the Amendment invests Congress with power to . . . adopt appropriate legislation for correcting the effects of such prohibited state law and state acts, and thus to render them effectually null, void, and innocuous. . . . It does not authorize Congress to create a code of municipal law for the regulation of private rights; but to provide modes of redress against the operation of state laws, and the action of state officers, executive or judicial, when these are subversive of the fundamental rights specified in the amendment. . . .

"An inspection of the law shows that it . . . proceeds ex directo to declare that certain acts committed by individuals shall be deemed offenses, and shall be prosecuted and punished by proceedings in the courts of the United States. It does not profess to be corrective of any constitutional wrong committed by the states; it . . . applies equally to case arising in states which have the justest laws respecting the personal rights of citizens, and whose authorities are ever ready to enforce such laws as to those which arise in states that may have violated the prohibition of the amendment. In other words, it steps into the domain of local jurisprudence, and lays down rules for the conduct of individuals in society towards each other. . . . [C]ivil rights, such as are guarantied by the constitution against state aggression, cannot be impaired by the wrongful acts of individuals, unsupported by state authority in the shape of laws, customs, or judicial or executive proceedings. The wrongful act of an individual, unsupported by any such authority, is simply a private wrong, or a crime of that individual. . . . An individual cannot deprive a man of his right to vote, to hold property, to buy and to sell, to sue in the courts, or to be a witness or a juror; he may, by force or fraud, interfere with the enjoyment of the right in a particular case; . . . but unless protected in these wrongful acts by some shield of state law or state authority, he cannot destroy or injure the right; he will only render himself amenable to satisfaction or punishment; and amenable therefor to the laws of the state where the wrongful acts are committed. [The] abrogation and denial of rights, for which the states alone were or could be responsible, was the great seminal and fundamental wrong which was intended to be remedied.

The dissent of Justice Harlan pointed out that

The basic doctrine of the *Civil Rights Cases*—that it is "state action" that is prohibited by the fourteenth amendment—has remained undisturbed. But the question of what constitutes "state action" has generated significant controversy. It is settled that the term comprehends statutes enacted by national, state and local legislative bodies and the official actions of all government officers. The more difficult problems arise when the label is sought to be affixed to the conduct of private individuals or groups with whom government is somehow "involved" or who allegedly exercise "government authority." Until recently, most efforts to hold such private individuals or groups to the constitutional responsibilities of the state have involved challenges to racial discrimination under the equal protection clause (some additional cases claiming denial of free speech). But, with the growth under the equal protection clause of the "suspect" classifications category and the expansion under the due process clause of the procedural rights that the state must afford persons before depriving them of liberty or property, an increasing number of cases (at least in the lower courts) have involved attempts to require "private" adherence to these constitutional obligations.

The highest court sixty–three years later in Marsh v. Alabama[2] held that "a State, consistently with the First and Fourteenth Amendments . . . (cannot) impose criminal punishment on a person who undertakes to distribute religious literature on the premises of a company-owned town contrary to the wishes of the town's management." The Court concluded:

Ownership does not always mean absolute dominion. The more an owner, for his advantage, opens up his property for use by the public in general, the more do his rights become circumscribed by the statutory and constitutional rights of those who use it. Thus, the owners of privately held bridges, ferries, turnpikes and rail-roads may not operate them as freely as a farmer does his farm. Since these facil-ities are built and operated primarily to benefit the public and since their operation is essentially a public function, it is subject to state regulation. And, though the issue is not directly analogous to the one before us, we do want to point out by way of illustration that such regulation may not result in an operation of these facilities, even by privately owned companies, which unconstitutionally interferes with and discriminates. . . .

Implicit in the First Amendment is the constitutional protection af-forded freedom of speech against infringement or abridgement by govern-ment, primarily the federal government. But the Fourteenth Amendment, as indicated above, applies that constitutional guarantee of freedom of speech against state and local governments.[3] In the latter instance, the free speech constitutional protection against state and local governments rests on the concept of "state action," as opposed to "private action." The principal query is whether the operation of "private property," such as a shopping center or shopping mall, qualifies as state action under the Fourteenth Amendment. Specifically, has the state given its endorsement or acquies-cence to the restraints or restrictions placed by the private owners of the shopping center or shopping mall upon the exercise of freedom of speech? In short, has the state acted positively in some way so that the otherwise private property owner and the state have become one entity?[4]

Part of the answer to these queries lies in an evaluation of two impor-tant basic factors: (1) the use and nature of the private property and (2) the nature of the speech activity. The Washington Supreme Court in Al-derwood Associates v. Washington Environmental Council[5] concluded that "as property becomes the functional equivalent of a downtown area or other public forum, reasonable speech activities become less of an intru-sion on the owner's autonomy interests. . . . When property is open to the public, the owner has a reduced expectancy of privacy and, as a cor-ollary, any speech activity is less threatening to the property's value."[6] On the second factor, the court echoed the holding that "the exercise of free speech is given great weight in the balance, because it is a preferred right." The concurring opinion of Justice Dolliver of the Washington Supreme Court, however, took exception to the majority opinion that the state con-stitution "may also be used by one individual against another" and de-scribed the majority opinion as "constitution-making by the judiciary of the most egregious sort." The concurring opinion reechoed the argument that the U.S. Constitution and the Bill of Rights, as well as state consti-tutions and bills of rights, were adopted "to protect individual rights against the government" and not against individuals. It was Justice Dolliver's view that "if the citizens of [the state of] Washington wish their constitution to be used as a sword against individuals in addition to being used as a shield against the actions of the State, there is a means by which this can be done."[7] However, Justice Dolliver agreed with the majority opinion that "the activity involved in this case was a reasonable restriction on the use of the Alderwood Mall by plaintiff and was not of such a nature as to constitute an uncompensated 'taking' of private property." The lone dissenting opinion of Justice Stafford would not allow persons "to go onto private property" because that activity "leaves owners of private property powerless to exclude them."

The First Amendment, interestingly, does not include an affirmative clause; the entire thrust of it is in the negative, as is evident in the prohibitions against abridgement of the rights of speech, press, assembly, and petition.[8] The inference to be gained from this fact is that the negative clause provides greater protection of these guaranteed rights. Yet it has been held that some state constitutional provisions, such as provisions in the California Constitution, may be broader in scope than the federal clause.[9]

Automobile license plates have provided a unique testing ground for state action under freedom of expression, according to *Insight* magazine (May 4, 1987).[10] George Maynard, a New Hampshire printer and a member of Jehovah's Witnesses, in 1975 taped over his New Hampshire license plate the state motto "Live Free or Die." He was arrested for defacing the plates, which were confiscated as evidence, and he was ticketed for not having license plates on his car. He paid a $75 fine and spent fifteen days in jail until the U.S. Supreme Court[11] agreed with him that he is not required by law to have his car used as "a mobile billboard for the State's ideological message," which was "Scenic New Hampshire." However, in State of Idaho v. Freese, where defendant taped over the Idaho license plate's words, "Famous Potatoes," the court ruled that the plate was constitutional but that the state law against covering up the advertisement was unconstitutional.[12] Other State license plate messages of note include Oklahoma's "Oklahoma is OK," Pennsylvania's "You've Got a Friend in Pennsylvania," North Carolina's "First in Flight," Wisconsin's "America's Dairyland," Arizona's "Grand Canyon State," Missouri's "Show-Me-State," Maine's "Vacationland," and New Mexico's "Land of Enchantment." The point is that the humble license plate has become a veritable battleground for First Amendment and Fourteenth Amendment rights.

4.1 THE RISE AND FALL OF THE PUBLIC FUNCTION DOCTRINE

It was in 1946 that the U.S. Supreme Court in Marsh v. Alabama[13] first articulated the public function doctrine that serves as the basis for state action under the Fourteenth amendment. The highest court was willing to find state action because it reflected the Court's political view or attitude toward the underlying constitutional claim. Here, the governing of a company town by private property interests was clearly a public function, bringing the restraint upon distribution of literature on the streets of the company town within the framework of the First Amendment. Explicit delegation of authority by the state was not necessary to invoke state action; mere acquiescence by the state is generally sufficient.[14] Justice Black wrote that the use of the property itself was the controlling feature for the company-owned town had all the physical characteristics of a municipality. Thus state action was present so as to invoke the First Amendment; the state had delegated a public function to a private entity. After find the requisite state action, the Court emphasized the need of citizens in a democracy to have access to uncensored information in order to make informed decisions. Furthermore, the large number of citizens living at that time in company-owned towns and the preferred position of speech[15] made it imperative that First Amendment rights be fully guaranteed.

This public function doctrine was given increased attention by the highest court in Amalgamated Food Employees v. Logan Valley Plaza, Inc.,[16] which dealt with the freedom of expression by picketing inside a private shopping center in Pennsylvania. The Court made both physical and functional comparisons between a company-owned town and a private shopping center and found them to be "strikingly similar." On the public functional level, it was determined that the extent of the public's invitation to the property was identical, and therefore speakers' access to both areas could not be denied. It was even determined that the private parking lot was part and parcel of the private shopping center, and the owners, performing a public function, could not immunize themselves from responsibility for protecting First Amendment rights. Admittedly, state action here was less pervasive than in a company-owned town, but the activity was still a public function based on the purpose and use of the property, the nature and extent of the public's invitation to enter and shop, and the relation between speech and the use of the private property.

On the other hand, where speech is unrelated to the commercial use of a shopping center, as in Lloyd Corp. v. Tanner,[17] the Court is reluctant to shield the dissemination of information. Here, speakers had attempted to distribute handbills protesting the Vietnam War, against the wishes of the shopping center owners. The federal district court in Oregon issued a permanent injunction restraining the private property owners from interfering with the distribution of handbills.[18] The Ninth U.S. Court of Appeals affirmed,[19] but the U.S. Supreme Court reversed by applying the public function doctrine comparing the company-owned town and the shopping center, concluding that a shopping center does not have all the attributes of a municipality. Furthermore, the public's invitation to enter and shop was not open-ended since the public was invited only to patronize the shops of the specific tenants within the shopping center. The distribution of handbills was declared to be unrelated to this invitation to enter and shop, for the handbilling could have occurred on public property, according to the Court. This 5–4 decision seemingly put a damper on the concept of a shopping center's performing a public function, though the dissenters were vehement in pointing out that the shopping center's private police force and the zoning ordinance designating the property as "an integral part of the community" satisfied the public function doctrine. In 1976 in Hudgens v. NLRB,[20] the highest court again dealt a blow to the public function of a shopping center that was picketed; the Court stated that the First Amendment did not protect access to private property.[21]

In 1980 in Robins v. Pruneyard Shopping Center,[22] the U.S. Supreme Court held that the free speech and petition provisions of the California Constitution protected a right of access in the common areas of a privately owned shopping mall. Reasonable restrictions on private property rights were justified in the light of the preferred right to freedom of speech.[23] And states may interpret their own constitutions to permit access to speakers on private property so long as the property owners are neither deprived of due process of law nor have their property "taken" witout just compensation.[24] A private college cannot prevent defendants from distributing leaflets outside a college building normally open to the public without being inconsistent with state constitutional rights of freedom of speech, assembly, and petition.[25] In Batchelder v. Allied Stores International,[26] the highest Massachusetts court held that a candidate for public office has a constitutional right to gather signatures supporting his nomination in a private shopping center. Curiously, the court based its determination not on free speech provisions of the commonwealth's constitution but on its guarantee of a free election, which it held did not have any state action prerequisite.

Perhaps the fall of the public function doctrine is best seen in the 1985 New York Court of Appeals decision in Shad Alliance v. Smith Haven Mall:[27] "To be sure, the shopping mall has taken on many of the attributes and functions of a public forum . . . but the characterization or the use of property is immaterial to the issue of whether action has been shown. Nor can the nature of the property transform a private actor into a public one."[28] Thus, according to many states like New York, the constitutional guarantees of free expression are only a shield against government and not a sword against individuals who are but trespassers with a cause.

4.2 CIVIL RIGHTS PROTECTION UNDER THE U.S. CODE

Section 1983 of the U.S. Code, Title 42, provides individuals with a private cause of action against any person, local (but not state) government, or federal government who, under color of state law, deprives the plaintiff or plaintiffs of rights guaranteed by federal law or the U.S. Constitution.[29] The statute traces its ancestry to the Ku Klux Klan Act of

1871,[30] an effort to protect newly freed black citizens from lawless activities of white citizens in the South. Its broad langauge has since its birth in 1871 offered a powerful tool to protect and preserve constitutional rights. (Congress in 1874 amended the statute to provide protection against deprivations of federal statutory rights.)[31] Individuals deprived of constitutional rights by person or persons acting under federal authority may also sue under the doctrine of Bivens v. Six Unknown Agents of the Federal Bureau of Narcotics.[32] Four other statutes under Title 42 of the U.S. Code provide for private redress for constitutional rights: the section 1981 (civil action for interference with "full and equal benefits of all laws for the security of persons and property"), section 1982 (civil action for interference with equal rights to "inherit, purchase, lease, sell, hold and convey" property), section 1895 (civil action for conspiracy to interfere with rights under the U.S. Constitution and federal laws), and section 1986 (civil action for failure to prevent the aforesaid conspiracy).[33] It should be observed that the Eleventh Amendment grants states sovereign immunity from federal court judgments under Title 42, section 1983.[34] Municipalities and local governments are not immune.[35]

Suits under section 1983 have been especially successful in striking down state action since 1961 when Monroe v. Pape[36] was decided by the U.S. Supreme Court. The phrase *under color of law* was construed broadly to encompass actions taken under pretense of law, and so actions against state officials' misusing their official positions were encouraged. The existence of state law remedies for civil rights violations does not preclude a federal civil suit for damages under section 1983.[37] Plaintiffs are not required to exhaust state remedies before bringing their cases to the federal court under section 1983. Reference to state laws in section 1988 of Title 42 is required for a section 1983 action if federal statutes are not precisely adapted to provide a remedy.[38]

A survey of relatively recent decisions points up the relatively few successful actions brought under section 1983 for First Amendment violations:

Albaum v. Carey[39] holding that allegations of fact were sufficient to show deprivation of right of free speech; abridgement of the right was effected under color of state statute.

Bart v. Telford,[40] pointing out that the allegation that after the public employee returned to work from a leave of absence while running for public office the mayor and three of his subordinates subjected her to a campaign of petty harassment in retaliation for her running for public office, stated a cause of action, for the campaign was motivated by plaintiff's views as a candidate.

Dennis v. County School Board,[41] alleging that the school superintendent and members of the school board acted under color of state law to punish a probationary teacher for her exercise of free speech.

Ghadiali v. Delaware State Medical Society,[42] declaring that members of the defendant society and municipal officers prevented the plaintiff, a retired medical doctor, academician, and scientific researcher, from disseminating information for lawful purposes and that injunctive relief was authorized for violation of First Amendment rights.

Gonzalez v. Benavides,[43] holding that the speech of the plaintiff, executive director of a community action agency, regarding the possibility that violations of regulations would result in loss of federal funds for poverty programs, whether the county commissioners' court had complied with regulations, and the authority of the county commissioners, raised issues of significant public concern, for purposes of determining whether speech was protected under the First Amendment; and dismissal of the plaintiff on the basis of such speech violated his right to free speech.

Hillis v. Stephen F. Austin State University,[44] to the effect that a nontenured art professor's criticism of the head of the art department did not lose its protection as a First Amendment right merely because it was a private expression directed at his superior.

Hughes v. Rizzo,[45] stating that the right of free speech may not be abridged even if the speakers are so unpopular as to give rise to fears of possible violence.

Jacobs v. Stratton,[46] declaring that where the decision not to renew the untenured plaintiff's teaching contract was based on his exercise of constitutionally protected freedom of expression, a cause of action was stated, though plaintiff could have been discharged for no reason or for a variety of other reasons.

Johnson v. Lincoln University,[47] holding that the plaintiff was terminated as a faculty member for his attempts to have other faculty members censured for allowing students to take advanced courses without passing requisites and for his criticism of the department chairman over the latter's academic standards. A cause of action for deprivation of First Amendment rights was stated.

Lewis v. Balckburn,[48] opining that the state magistrate's criticism of a court clerk's delegation of microfilming duties to the plaintiff was not a proper basis for plaintiff's dismissal annd plaintiff's retaliatory speech entitled her to relief under section 1983.

Providence Journal Co. v. McCoy,[49] holding that the ordinance and resolutions of the city council denying the right of any person to examine city records of tax cancellations or tax abatements without the express permission of the city council were invalid as in abridgement of freedom of speech.

Among the relatively recent decisions denying relief for First Amendment violations may be cited the following:

Adamian v. Lombardi,[50] holding that a professor who played a prominent role in unauthorized student protest demonstrations during school hours on school property, such as leading raucous catcalls at the university president, attempting to halt the state governor's motorcade, and otherwise disrupting university functions, was not discharged for violation of his freedom of speech activities.

Anderson v. Evans,[51] to the effect that the interest of the state, as employer, in limiting the employee's freedom of expression was significantly greater than any interest the state might have in similarly limiting expression by a member of the general public; therefore, the state employer's action against the employee did not amount to a constitutional violation of freedom of expression requiring remedial action.

Anderson v. Randall Park Mall Corporation,[52] declaring that no state action occurred when plaintiff was detained (for making noises and impeding crowd control) by security guards employed by the operator of a private shopping mall.

Curtis v. Russo & Mastracco, Inc.,[53] stating that the large supermarket open to the public where plaintiff was arrested for union activity was private property, and therefore the situs did not attest to the requisite state action, nor did the arrest by police acting in good faith provide the requisite state action; furthermore, there was no constitutional right of speech in privately owned places, and the claim for malicious prosecution did not present any deprivation of rights, privileges, or immunities secured by the U.S. Constitution or laws of the United States.

Gahr v. Trammel,[54] holding that a discharged Arkansas teacher had fair opportunity to litigate his claim in state court for an alleged First Amendment claim arising from his discharge in retaliation for his alleged accusations against the school superintendent and other school personnel.

Gearhart v. Thorne,[55] opining that First Amendment protection was not invoked by a state employee's grievance relating to false charges of his ineptitude, which were "matters only of personal interest."

Hearn v. Hudson,[56] holding that face-to-face threats of harm addressed to children were plainly without constitutional protection under freedom of speech.

Russ v. White,[57] stating that the college dean (who was terminated) had publicly expressed his anger, making physical threats toward other people with whom he had to work, and publicly made derogatory comments about his supervisor and other administrative personnel; the college dean had no constitutionally protected right to express himself in this unbusinesslike and unreasonable manner, and there was no termination by reason of protected freedom of expression.

Shaw v. Board of Trustees,[58] holding that although the college faculty members had a right to voice their disagreement with changes in the tenure system, their discharge for violating the policy manual by failing to take part in two college functions, in which their participation was mandatory, did not violate their First Amendment rights; their conduct went far beyond clear speech and into the realm of breach of express obligations of employment.

Solmitz v. Maine School Administrative District,[59] pointing out that the right of students to receive information as a component of free speech was not violated by the school's cancellation of speech at the school by a homosexual; the cancellation was based on a reasonable concern by the defendant for safety, order, and security following a telephoned bomb threat.

Whaley v. Cavanagh,[60] holding that a placard displayer's First Amendment rights were not violated by police regulations against obstruction of a public sidewalk on which pedestrian traffic was heavy.

Yoggerst v. Stewart,[61] providing for limited good faith immunity for state agency officials who reprimanded the plaintiff for making remarks to a coworker that conveyed her pleasure at the impending demise of the director of employment because the remarks were deemed not to be matters of public import but merely an expression of her personal dissatisfaction with the director.

Section 1983 has been characterized as a remedial statute that does not, ipso facto, create new rights but instead provides a mechanism by which established rights may be enforced and vindicated. The U.S. Supreme Court in 1983 in Smith v. Wade[62] indicated that section 1983 "creates a species of tort liability," but at the same time in City of Los Angeles v. Lyons,[63] the Court laid down the strict rules for injunctive relief as well as for punitive damages. Earlier, in Carey v. Piphus,[64] the Court had ruled that in the absence of proof of actual injury for a violation of constitutional rights, only nominal damages could be awarded: "Although mental and emotional distress caused by the denial of procedural due process itself is compensable under Section 1983, we hold that neither the likelihood of such injury nor the difficulty of proving it is so great as to justify awarding compensatory damages without proof that such injury actually was caused."[65]

Immunity from civil damages liability under section 1983 has been given not only to the state itself[66] but also to state judges[67] and state prosecutors.[68] Municipalities are immune only from section 1983 punitive damages.[69] In Supreme Court of Virginia v. Consumers Union,[70] state legislators were rewarded with absolute immunity from injunctive and declaratory judgment remedies, as well under section 1983.

NOTES

1. 109 US 3, 3 S Ct 18 (1883).
2. 326 US 501, 66 S Ct 276 (1946).
3. See generally Glennon & Nowak, "A Functional Analysis of the Fourteenth Amendment," 1976 Supp Sup Ct Rev 221, at p. 228.
4. See 18 Gonzaga L Rev 81 (1982–1983) at p. 92 et seq.
5. 635 P2d 108 (Wash., 1981).
6. On the right of privacy, see Warren Freedman, The Right of Privacy in the Computer Age (Quorum Books, 1987).
7. Infra note 5 at p. 119.
8. See 26 Hastings L J 481 (1974) at pp. 493–96.
9. See Dailey v. Superior Court, 44 P 458 (Cal., 1896), and Wilson v. Superior Court, 532 P2d 116 (Cal., 1975).
10. At p. 23.
11. Wooley v. Maynard, 430 US 705 (1977).
12. —P2d — (Unreported, Ida., 1980).

13. 326 US 501 (1946).

14. See 46 Albany L Rev 1501 (1982) at p. 1505.

15. See United States v. Carolene Products Co., 304 US 144 (1938) at pp. 152–53.

16. 391 US 308 (1968).

17. 407 US 551 (1972).

18. 308 F Supp 128 (Ore., 1970).

19. 446 F2d 545 (9th Cir., 1971).

20. 424 US 507 (1976).

21. Other examples of courts finding no state action include Amalgamated Clothing Workers v. Wonderland Shopping Center, 122 NW2d 785 (Mich., 1963); Woodland v. Michigan Citizens Lobby, 378 NW2d 337 (Mich., 1985); Shad Alliance v. Smith Haven Mall, 498 NYS2d 99, 488 NE2d 1211 (N.Y., 1985); State v. Felmet, 273 SE2d 708 (N.C., 1981); and Cologne v. Westfarms Associates, 469 A2d 1201 (Conn., 1984).

22. 447 US 74 (1980).

23. Infra note 14 at p. 1511.

24. See chapter 5 to this book, especially section 5.4.

25. Commonwealth of Pennsylvania v. Tate, 432 A2d 1382 (Pa., 1982).

26. 445 NE2d 590 (Mass., 1983).

27. 66 NY2d 496, 488 NE2d 1211 (1985).

28. Id. at p. 502 and at pp. 1217–18.

29.

Every person who, under color of any statute, ordinance, regulation, custom, or usage, of any State or Territory or the District of Columbia, subjects, or causes to be subjected, any citizen of the United States or other person within the jurisdiction thereof to the deprivation of any rights, privileges, or immunities secured by the Constitution and laws, shall be liable to the party injured in an action at law, suit in equity, or other proper proceeding for redress. For the purpose of this section, any Act of Congress applicable exclusively to the District of Columbia shall be considered to be a statute of the District of Columbia.

30. 17 Stat 13 (1871).

31. See Maine v. Thiboutot, 448 US 1 (1980) at pp. 7–8.

32. 403 US 388 (1971).

33. See generally 11 Hofstra L Rev 557 (1983).

34. See Quern v. Jordan, 440 US 332 (1979).

35. See Monell v. Department of Social Services, 436 US 658 (1978).

36. 365 US 167 (1961).

37. See 20 Tulsa L J 1 (1984) at p. 3.

38. Id. at p. 6.

39. 283 F Supp 3 (SDNY, 1968).

40. 677 F2d 622 (7th Cir., 1982).

41. 582 F Supp 536 (Va., 1984).

42. 28 F Supp 841 (Del., 1939).

43. 774 F2d 1295 (5th Cir., 1985): "The defendants concede that Gonzalez was fired because of his speech. . . . we believe the importance of the programs at stake raised the issue to a matter of significant public concern. . . . Compliance with the regulations by the Commissioners' Court is a matter of significant public concern."

44. 665 F2d 547 (5th Cir., 1982), reh den 669 F2d 729 (5th Cir., 1982), cert den 457 US 1106 (1982).

45. 282 F Supp 881 (Pa., 1968).

46. 615 P2d 982 (N.M., 1982).

47. 776 F2d 443 (3d Cir., 1985).

48. 734 F2d 1000 (4th Cir., 1984).

49. 94 F Supp 186 (R.I., 1950), aff 190 F2d 760 (1st Cir., 1951), cert den 342 US 894 (1951).

50. 608 F2d 1224 (9th Cir., 1979): "Professor Adamian was not denied freedom of speech, nor of assembly, nor equal protection."

51. 660 F2d 153 (4th Cir., 1981).

52. 571 F Supp 1173 (ND Ohio, 1983):

To maintain an action under 42 USC 1983, a party must establish two elements: (1) the deprivation of a right or privilege secured by the Constitution and laws of the United States, and (2) that the deprivation occurred under color of State law. . . . Anderson's allegation that the security guards acted under color of State law by virtue of their State licensing and their authority to detain shoplifters, is not well taken. . . . Anderson was not placed in police custody, nor were police ever called. . . . Clearly, State action cannot be found where, as here, the Ohio statutes do not compel detention of trespassers or shoplifters.

53. 413 F Supp 804 (Va., 1976):

A shopping center or other similarly situated privately owned facilities are not the functional equivalents of a public municipal facility. Therefore, traditional constitutional protections for purposes of the 14th Amendment and Section 1983 do not attach to activities conducted in shopping centers. . . . Plaintiff was not discriminated against on the basis of race or by exercising his First Amendment liberties. . . . The pleadings are absent any averment that the State acted in other than a neutral manner. . . . The State action nexus of the Fourteenth Amendment was not met. . . . There is no absolute right under the Constitution to be free from all arbitrary and capricious discrimination in a privately-owned establishment that is open to the public.

54. 796 F2d 1063 (8th Cir., 1986).

55. 768 F2d 1072 (9th Cir., 1985).

56. 549 F Supp 949 (Va., 1982).

57. 541 F Supp 888 (Ark., 1981), aff 680 F2d 47 (6th Cir., 1981).

58. 549 F2d 929 (4th Cir., 1976). The lone dissenting opinion opined that

Shaw and Winn were discharged because they acted in concert with their fellows to protest a college policy. . . . Though camouflaged as discharges for breaking a college rule, the college's retaliation . . . violates the precepts [of the First Amendment]. . . . The right of Shaw and Winn to protest the college's employment policies was protected by the First Amendment. They did not forfeit this protection, for their protest neither impaired their own work nor interfered with the operation of the school.

59. 495 A2d 812 (Maine, 1985).

60. 237 F Supp 900 (Cal., 1963), aff 341 P2d 295 (Cal., 1964), cert den 382 US 872 (1964).

61. 571 F Supp 68 (Ill., 1983).

62. 461 US 30 (1983) at p. 34.

63. 461 US 95 (1983).

64. 435 US 247 (1978).

65. Id. at p. 264.

66. Note the Eleventh Amendment, and see Quern v. Jordan, 440 US 332 (1979).

67. Pierson v. Ray, 386 US 547 (1967).

68. Imbler v. Pachtman, 424 US 409 (1976).

69. City of Newport v. Fact Concerts, Inc., 453 US 247 (1981).

70. 446 US 247 (1981).

5

Protection of Property Rights Under the Fifth and Fourteenth Amendments

Property rights and their protection is the theme of many recent state court decisions that involve guarantees of freedom of expression. The 1985 New York Court of Appeals case of Shad Alliance v. Smith Haven Mall[1] is but a reflection of the prevailing view that individual property rights merit protection under the Fifth and the Fourteenth amendments, even in the face of superior constitutional guarantees of freedom of expression under the First Amendment, as delineated by the U.S. Supreme Court in its 1980 landmark opinion in Robins v. Pruneyard Shopping Center.[2] That epochal decision favors protection of property interests consonant with the state's ability to determine how that property should be used. Above all, the property owner's absolute right to control and use his or her property must yield to such paramount state interests as the implementation of state social and economic policies,[3] the exercise of other constitutional rights,[4] and the state's abiding concern for health, safety, and public welfare.[5]

The "fairness doctrine"[6] applied to radio and television broadcasting amounts to an infringement on the property rights of the radio and television proprietors, it can be argued. Chief Judge David Bazelon of the District of Columbia U.S. Court of Appeals, almost twenty years ago, in Banzaf v. Federal Communications Commission,[7] had occasion to weigh the property right in sizing up the fairness doctrine as applied to cigarette advertising and its impact on the First Amendment:

The speech which might conceivably be "chilled" by this ruling barely qualifies as constitutionally protected "speech." It is established that some utterances fall outside the pale of First Amendment concern. . . . Product advertising is at least less rigorously protected than other forms of speech. . . . Promoting the sale of a product is not ordinarily associated with any of the interests the First Amendment seeks to protect. As a rule, it does not affect the political process, does not contribute to the exchange of ideas, does not provide information on matters of public importance, and is not, except perhaps for the ad man, a form of individual self-expression. It is rather a form of merchandising subject to limitation for public purposes like other business practices. . . . In any event, the danger that even this marginal "speech" will be significantly chilled as a result of the ruling (in favor of the "fairness doctrine") is probably itself marginal. . . . Even if some valued speech is inhibited by the ruling, the First Amendment gain is greater than the loss. A primary First Amendment policy has been to foster the widest possible debate and dissemination of information on matters of public importance. That policy has been pursued by a general hostility toward any deterrents to free expression. . . . If the fairness doctrine cannot withstand First Amendment scrutiny, the reason is that to insure a balanced presentation of controversial issues may be to insure no presentation, or no vigorous presentation, at all. . . . We think the purpose of rugged debate is served, not hindered, by an attempt to redress the balance. . . . A political system which assigns vital decisions to individual free choice assumes a well-informed citizenry.[8]

Broadcasters, zealous of their property interests in the airwaves, seek First Amendment protection against government regulation, which includes the fairness doctrine. Opponents point out that the broadcasting industry has, at most, a limited property interest in the airwaves, which in reality are part of the public trust. The U.S. Supreme Court in 1969 in Red Lion Broadcasting Co. v. FCC[9] ruled that it was "idle to posit an unabridgeable First Amendment right to broadcast comparable to the right of every individual to speak, write, or publish."[10]

5.1 PUBLIC ACCESS TO PRIVATE FORUMS

Property that performs a substantial public function[11] may also retain private characteristics. Therefore courts, in addressing the conflict between speech rights and property rights, must carefully examine the character of the property in order to balance the burden the property owner puts on freedom of speech against the burden on the owner's property right. (Note that the Fifth Amendment forbids the "taking"[12] of property without just compensation,[13] and the Fourteenth Amendment forbids states to confiscate property without due process of law.)[14] When the property bears virtually all the characteristics of public property, the balance must favor freedom of expression. However, there is a caveat, as expressed by the dissenting opinion of Justice Stafford in Alderwood Associates v. Washington Environmental Council:[15] "One problem with the constitutional interpretation by both the majority and the concurrence is that neither seems to have a logical stopping point. Counsel for defendant-petitioners conceded that . . . if a private person's home was on the busiest corner of the city and hence the best available place from which to gather signatures, the collector's alleged constitutional right would compel the homeowner to allow a card table to be set up on his front lawn."[16]

This apparent lack of a logical stopping point mandates scrutiny of the shopping center or shopping mall itself. The Alderwood Mall is a shopping center containing over 1 million square feet of retail floor space on 110 acres of land with over 6,000 parking spaces for the daily flow of 40,000 automobiles. The Alderwood Mall is perhaps five times larger than Pruneyard Shopping Center featured in the Robins case.[17] In the Logan Valley case,[18] the U.S. Supreme Court, in also protecting freedom of speech, was, however, content merely to find that shopping centers are functionally equivalent to "downtown business blocks"[19] and sites for protection of the rights.

Other examples of private properties that take on the hue of public forums are nursing homes and hospitals, migrant labor camps, company-owned towns, residential complexes, corporate office buildings, and even private university campuses. Nursing homes and hospitals provide the whole spectrum of municipal services to their residents, who have limited access to outside information, and therefore their right to free speech is paramount.[20] Migrant labor camps and company-owned towns are, on the other hand, less open for freedom of expression, and free access to such places must be mandated by the courts.[21] Here again the places provide all municipal services, serving a truly public function, which means that freedom of speech takes precedence over the property rights of the owners. Residential complexes, including private housing developments, frequently provide most municipal services and therefore are generally precluded from abridging the freedom of expression, as illustrated in Martin v. Struthers,[22] in which the U.S. Supreme Court, upholding free speech, refused to permit the housing authority to decide for its residents whether to tolerate solicitation on the property of the residential complex. But where the housing development, condominium, and cooperative is private and perhaps even located on streets and byways that are privately owned, federal or state protection of free expression is often precluded.[23] But in Laguna Publishing Co. v. Golden Rains Foundation,[24] the California appellate court held that the discriminatory exclusion from Leisure World, a private residential development, of a giveaway newspaper violated the California constitutional provisions on freedom of speech and freedom of the press. The court found that Leisure World was functionally equivalent to a municipality, although the residential complex was not open to the public; therefore state action was present because the community had invoked the state trespass law in a discriminatory manner. But as a private community, Leisure World could keep out all newspapers as long as there was no discriminatory treatment of newspapers. The end result appears to be frightening for the future protection of freedom of expression as more and more private residential communities supplant public forums of the inner city. Professor Louis Henkin wrote about fifteen years ago, "The freedom of speech, press and religion require extraordinary judicial protection against invasions even for the public good, because of their place at the foundation of democracy and because of the unreliability of the political process in regard to them."[25]

Corporate office buildings and office complexes have generally been denied free speech access[26] although they are analogous to shopping centers and shopping malls in the sense that there is an open commercial invitation to the public to enter. In Commonwealth v. Hood,[27] the highest Massachusetts court held that the distribution of antinuclear leaflets in an outdoor courtyard on the private office building premises was unprotected by the state constitution; the premises here were not used by the public at large. A ban on the distribution of advertising circulars in the lobby of a private bank was also sustained in Rains v. Mercantile National Bank.[28]

Private university campuses have been the sites in New Jersey and in Pennsylvania for extending protection for freedom of expression. In State of New Jersey v. Schmid,[29] Princeton University had barred an uninvited solicitor from the campus; but Princeton's relationship with the state was too tenuous to warrant Princeton's acts as state action. The court predicated its ruling on the New Jersey Constitution, which independently provided greater protection than the First Amendment "against unreasonably restrictive or oppressive conduct on the part of private entities that have otherwise assumed a constitutional obligation not to abridge the individual exercise of such freedom because of the public use of their property."[30] The New Jersey court reasoned that "one of the most important functions performed by State constitutional bills of rights which is not performed by the federal constitution is the protection of citizens against private abridgement as well as the oppression of the State."[31] The court further observed that Princeton regulations declared that "free inquiry and free expression within the academic community are indispensable to the achievement of goals" and that Princeton had invited the public to use its property, facilities, and resources in order to fulfill its educational goals. Therefore the dissemination of political pamphlets was not incompatible with the university's goals or the public or private uses of its property.[32] Princeton's regulations barring the uninvited solicitor were declared to be unreasonable and not enforceable (which regulations Princeton later amended).

The Pennsylvania Supreme Court in Commonwealth v. Tate[33] was concerned with nonstudents' distributing leaflets on privately owned Muhlenberg College campus. Again the state court upheld freedom of expression on the basis of the Pennsylvania Constitution and in reliance on the state statute on trespass, which contained an affirmative defense when property is open to the public at the time of entry and the trespasser complies with all lawful conditions for access.[34] Muhlenberg College clearly held itself out to the public as a "community resource and cultural center," according to the court; and although the college has the right to regulate activity on campus, it acted unreasonably in selectively denying citizens the privilege to distribute pamphlets on campus.

5.2 EXTENSION TO ELECTRONIC AND PRINT MEDIA

Property rights protected as against free expression also finds root in the electronic and print media, which are privately owned and managed. Must these property owners allow use of their facilities for communication of certain kinds of messages? A critical difference from other property owners is that owners of newspapers and broadcasting stations are themselves in the business of communication. If access to their facilities is sought by persons in the name of freedom of speech, the conflict is between persons competing for recognition of their First Amendment rights. The property rights of the electronic and print media are on the back burner; each side challenges the other for supremacy on freedom of expression grounds.[35]

Courts have somewhat resolved the conflict by holding that the electronic and print media have no obligation to provide for First Amendment rights of others, but these property owners nevertheless may be imposed upon in the interest of not obstructing the First Amendment rights of others. The electronic media operate their facilities, it is said, for the public interest, convenience, and necessity. Under the fairness doctrine, broadcasters are required, when dealing with controversial public issues, to present a diversity of views.[36] Thus members of the public theoretically have a right to use the electronic media for circulation of their views and opinions on given issues, as selected by the electronic media. Equal opportunities for candidates for public office are delineated in section 315 of the Federal Communications Act. In Red Lion Broadcasting Co. v. FCC,[37] the U.S. Supreme Court in 1969 rejected the argument that regulations of the electronic media infringed upon the freedom of speech of the broadcasters:

As far as the First Amendment is concerned, those who are licensed stand no better than those to whom licenses are refused. A license permits broadcasting, but the licensee has no constitutional right to be the one who holds the license to monopolize a radio frequency to the exclusion of his fellow citizens. There is nothing in the First Amendment which prevents the Government from requiring a licensee to share his frequency with others and to conduct himself as a proxy or fiduciary with obligations to present those views and voices which are representative of this community and which would otherwise, by necessity, be barred from the airwaves. . . . It is the right of the viewers and listeners, not the right of the broadcasters, which is paramount. . . . It is the purpose of the First Amendment to preserve an uninhibited marketplace of ideas in which truth will ultimately prevail.[38]

Four years later, in Columbia Broadcasting System v. Democratic National Committee,[39] the highest court, however, favored the broadcasters on the issue of whether a claimed First Amendment right of members of the public to purchase time for editorial advertisements on issues of current controversy should take priority over the claimed First Amendment right of broadcasters to have a policy of not selling airtime for such editorial advertisements.[40] And in 1978, the U.S. Supreme Court in FCC v. Pacifica Foundation[41] upheld the authority of the FCC to penalize a radio broadcaster for airing an "indecent" but not "obscene" broadcast.

On March 23, 1987, the highest court, in Wilkinson v. Jones,[42] in a memorandum decision, affirmed the ruling by the Tenth U.S. Court of Appeals that the Utah Cable Television Programming Decency Act of 1983 violated both the First Amendment and a 1984 federal statute that preempted, with narrow exceptions, state and local regulation of cable programming. The Utah act delineated visual or verbal depiction or description of human sexual or excretory organs or functions, including exposure of male or female genitals, pubic area, buttocks, or any portion of the female breast below the top of the nipple as "indecent material"; the standard applied was the "average person applying contemporary community standards for cable television . . . [who] would find [it] is presented in a patently offensive way for the time, place, manner and context."[43] The court found that this delineation was unconstitutionally vague and overbroad. (Violation of the Utah act constituted a nuisance punishable by fines and money forfeitures.) The federal district trial court had found for the plaintiffs on the basis of the federal preemption of state regulation of the content of cable television programming, although cable operators may still be held liable by a state for violating "obscenity . . . or other similar laws".[44] The Utah act was found by the federal district court to go beyond that limited power and was "unconstitutionally overbroad and vague, and void on its face."[45] In affirming, the federal appellate court dwelled upon the issue of the cable companies' entitlement to attorneys' fees under Title 42, section 1988, of the U.S. Code and ruled that a party's ability to bring a civil rights suit without a fee award is not "special circumstances" rendering the fee award unjust or deniable. A concurring opinion by Judge Baldock stressed his disagreement with the court's ruling on federal preemption, as well as with the court's view that the First Amendment forecloses the regulation of indecency on cable television, "provided that the regulation is a time, place, and manner restriction and exists for the protection of minors." He cited the Utah statute[46] as "void for vagueness" because "without more, would cause people of common intelligence to guess at the meaning of indecency and differ as to the law's application."

Thus, it would appear that the states have no constitutional authority to regulate patently offensive, indecent broadcasting unless the broadcasting is obscene.

The print media, unlike the electronic media including broadcasting, are not licensed or regulated, for print media are considered to be protected under the freedom of press provision of the First Amendment. Professor Lucas A. Powe, Jr., in his 1987 treatise, *American Broadcasting and the First Amendment*,[47] urged that print media and broadcasting be treated alike. His persuasive and slashing criticism of federal regulation of broadcasting attests to what he calls favoritism, imposition of white middle-class ethics upon viewers and listeners, and political manipulation. Powe insists that broadcasting and print are no different and that both should be equally protected by the First Amendment. Justice Marshall, in his dissenting opinion in Lloyd Corp. v. Tanner,[48] did not observe the difference, if any, as he recounted that "for many persons who do not have easy access to television, radio, the major newspapers, and other forms of mass media, the only way they can express themselves to a broad range of citizens on issues of general public concern is to picket, to handbill, or to utilize other free or relatively inexpensive means of communication."[49] The point is well taken by the Fifth U.S. Court of Appeals' pronouncement in 1986 in Rankin v. McPherson.[50] The defendant clerk-typist in a Texas constable's office was fired when she expressed her wish that President Reagan be shot again after he survived the Hinckley bullet. The prosecutor argued that she should be denied free speech protection because the government's interest in promoting employee morale outweighed any First Amendment issue. But the court determined that her utterance must be protected for it was her means or her way to express herself on the public issue. The U.S. Supreme Court affirmed.

The state of New York sought by statute to protect journalists' sources and materials from subpoenas in a so-called shield law, but the New York Court of Appeals in a 4–3 decision in Knight-Ridder Broadcasting, Inc, v. Greenberg[51] construed the statute as protecting only confidential information and confidential sources: "Where the interpretation of a statute is well settled and accepted across the State, it is as much a part of the enactment as if incorporated into the language of the act itself. Consequently, any intention to change such a well-established rule must emanate from the Legislature." The majority of the court had observed that the lower New York courts had consistently construed the shield law as limited to confidential information and confidential sources. The three dissenters argued that the majority of the court had inserted "confidentiality" into the statute that contained no such requisite.[52] Thus, the shield for journalists was severely restricted and the First Amendment rights of journalists somewhat impaired.

5.3 TAKING OF PROPERTY AND JUST COMPENSATION

There are two basic constitutional limitations on state infringement on property rights: the Fifth Amendment, which prohibits the taking of private property without just compensation, and the Fourteenth Amendment, which bans deprivation of property without due process of law. As viewed by the U.S. Supreme Court in the Pruneyard Shopping Center case,[53] "The guaranty of due process . . . demands only that the law shall not be unreasonable, arbitrary and capricious, and that the means selected shall have a real and substantial relation to the objective sought to be obtained."[54] Speech activity or expression activity can impair the value or use of property, as demonstrated in Kaiser Aetna v. United States,[55] where the U.S. Supreme Court declared that the depriving of residents of a private community of their right to exclude others interferes with their reasonable, investment-backed expectations constituted a taking of property without just compensation in violation of the Fifth Amendment. This "taking" clause clearly applies to the states under the Fourteenth Amendment. In Alderwood Associates v. Washington Environmental Council,[56] the Washington Supreme Court found that the solicitation of signatures at the private shopping center was not an activity

where the speech activity so affects the value or use of the shopping center as to constitute a "taking" of the mall owner's property. . . . Petitioners' activities were neither disruptive nor offensive. In fact, they had been allowed in other shopping centers of similar size within our State. Those other mall operators had granted permission on the condition that the activities be orderly and not interfere with business activities. Petitioners agreed to those conditions, indicating that the activity was one susceptible to reasonable regulation and could be performed in a manner that accommodated both parties' needs.

The same state court opined: "Reading our State constitution to allow this type of activity does not violate due process. . . . Signature gathering in a shopping mall furthers the exchange of ideas. . . . It thus is a reasonable means of serving two important State interests." The one dissenting opinion observed that "citizens have nowhere been given the right, either constitutionally or statutorily, to collect . . . signatures on private property."

In the Pruneyard case in 1980,[57] the U.S. Supreme Court measured the alleged taking of private property by reference to whether the requirement of access "forces some people alone to bear public burdens which, in all fairness and justice, should be borne by the public as a whole."[58] The Court viewed the "character of the governmental action," its economic impact on the interests of the property owners, and its interference with reasonable investment-backed opportunities and expectations. After applying these criteria, the Court concluded that since there had been no taking under the Fifth Amendment, there was no loss to measure. The property owners were still free to establish time, place, and manner regulations[59] on "expressive" activities of every nature. Interestingly, it is generally the courts that are institutionally entrusted with protection of the utility of speech because the legislatures are frequently unresponsive to the politically powerless.[60]

Actual measurement of the taking relates to a diminution-of-value test, as first developed by Justice Oliver Wendell Holmes in 1922 in Pennsylvania Coal Co. v. Mahon.[61] The extent to which the economic value of the property had been diminished by the taking was the measure of damages.[62] In the Pruneyard Shopping Center case, the 1980 U.S. Supreme Court listed the factor relevant to the determination: "The character of the governmental action, its economic impact, . . . when the regulation goes too far."[63] The National Film Board of Canada experienced a labeling of its films by the U.S. government as "propaganda," and a U.S. film distributor sustained damages to his "ability to obtain re-election and to practice his profession" in Keene v. United States, decided by the U.S. Supreme Court on April 28, 1987. The measurement of the taking was not possible, but the highest court ruled that the governmental action pursuant to the Foreign Agents Registration Act of 1938 (amended in 1942 and 1966) was constitutional. It appears that in 1982, the National Film Board of Canada had submitted sixty-two films and videotapes to the U.S. Department of Justice for review under the act. If the films and videotapes are "political propaganda," they must carry a notice of what country or agent produced the material, which is to be labeled propaganda. The U.S. Department of Justice reviewed five of the films and videotapes and concluded that three of the five films dealt with acid rain and nuclear war and were therefore political propaganda. Justice John Paul Stevens was of the opinion that the use of the term *propaganda* "has no pejorative connotation," but three dissenting opinions stated that the term was not neutral, and therefore applying it to the films was an infringement of First Amendment rights of freedom of expression. Justice Stevens stressed "the respect we normally owe to the Legislature's power to define the terms that it uses in legislation," although he was aware of the "potential misunderstanding" that could arise from the widespread popular assumption that the word means "a form of slanted, misleading speech that does not merit serious attention." In holding that the law placed "no burden on protected expression," he acknowledged that some people might suspect a film that must be registered with the Justice Department; but "there is no evidence that this suspicion—to the degree it exists—has had the effect of Government censorship." The dissent of Justice Harry Blackmun felt that such "governmental disparagement" of speech clearly violated the First Amendment; he stated that the majority's definition of *political propaganda* strains credulity, for the word is definitely not a neutral classification. Indeed, the Foreign Agents Registration Act defined the word as follows: "The term 'political propaganda' includes an oral, visual, graphic, written, pictorial, or other communication or expression by any person . . . which is reasonably adapted to, or which the person disseminating the same believes will, or which he intends to, prevail upon, indoctrinate, convert, induce, or in any other way influence a recipient or any section of the public within the United States with reference to political or public interest, policies, or relations of a government or of a foreign country or a foreign political party or with reference to the foreign policies of the United States."[64]

In First English Evangelical Lutheran Church of Glendale v. County of Los Angeles,[65] the U.S. Supreme Court on June 9, 1987, extended the rule that persons whose property is taken by the government are entitled to just compensation, even for temporary regulatory takings. Here, the plaintiff church had bought land in 1957 for recreational purposes; in 1977, a forest fire scorched the area, and the next year a flash flood denuded its hills. The county then adopted an ordinance prohibiting construction of any building or structure along the banks of the river. The church sued for loss of use of its property. At the outset of its opinion, the highest court opined: "We accordingly have no occasion to decide whether the ordinance at issue actually denied appellant all use of its property or whether the county might avoid the conclusion that a compensable taking had occurred by establishing the denial of all use was insulated as part of the State's authority to enact safety regulations. . . . These questions of course must remain open for decision on the remand we direct today." It has been recognized that a taking need not be physical to deprive an owner of property; a regulation preventing the use of that property may have the same effect.[66] But even the rescission of the regulation still entitles the owner to temporary regulatory compensation. According to the Court, "Government action other than acquisition of title, occupancy, or physical invasion can be a 'taking,' and therefore a de facto exercise of the power of eminent domain, where the effects completely deprive the owner of all or most of his interest in the property." (But there is no right to the profitable use of one's property.)[67] The Court did not deal with "the case of normal delays in obtaining building permits, changes in zoning ordinances, variances, and the like which are not before us."

NOTES

1. 488 NE2d 1211 (N.Y., 1985), 498 NYS2d 99 (1985).
2. 447 US 74 (1980).
3. See Lombard v. Louisiana, 373 US (1963).
4. Cf. Shelley v. Kramer, 334 US 1 (1948); note 10 Golden Gate U L Rev 805 (1980) at p. 833.
5. Id.
6. See generally 37 U Cin L Rev 447 (1968).
7. 405 F2d 1082 (DC Cir., 1968).
8. According to the court, radio and television revenues from cigarette advertising in the late 1960s totaled nearly $300 million annually, more than 7 percent of all television advertising revenue.

9. 395 US 367 (1969).

10. See New York Times (April 5, 1987) at p. E28. In late December 1987 Congress in passing its vital legislative package on the budget omitted favorable reference to the "fairness doctrine," and thus the "fairness doctrine" is dead!

11. See section 4.1 herein.

12. See section 5.3.

13. See Chicago, B&O Railroad Co. v. Chicago, 166 US 226 (1987).

14. See Nebbia v. New York, 291 US 502 (1934).

15. 635 P2d 108 (Wash., 1981).

16. Id. at p. 254.

17. 447 US 17 (1980).

18. 391 US 308 (1968).

19. Id. at pp. 319, 325.

20. See generally 37 Syracuse L Rev 1 (1986).

21. See 55 Chi-Kent L Rev 285 (1979).

22. 319 US 141 (1943).

23. See Watchtower Bible & Tract Society v. Metropolitan Life Insurance, Inc., 79 NE2d 433 (N.Y., 1948), cert den 335 US 886 (1948), which held that a Jehovah's Witness did not have the right to canvass residents of Parkchester, a community of 35,000. To the same effect is Hall v. Commonwealth of Virginia, 49 SE2d 369 (Va., 1948).

24. 182 Cal Rptr 813 (1982), app dism 459 1192 (1982).

25. 74 Columbia L Rev 1410 (1974) at p. 1429.

26. See Bellemead Development Corp. v. Schneider, 472 A2d 170 (N.J., 1983), and Rains v. Mercantile National Bank, 559 SW2d 121 (Tex Civ App., 1980).

27. 452 NE2d 188 (Mass., 1983).

28. Infra note 26.

29. 423 A2d 615 (N.J., 1980), app dism sub nom Princeton University v. Schmid, 455 US 100 (1982).

30. Id. at p. 628.

31. Id.

32. Id. at p. 631.

33. 432 A2d 1382 (Pa., 1981).

34. Section 3503(b) and (c) of 18 Pa Cons Stat Ann.

35. See generally 58 Wash L Rev 587 (1983).

36. Infra notes 9 and 10; also see In the Matter of the Mayflower Broadcasting Co., 8 FCC 333 (1941).

37. 395 US 367 (1969).

38. Id. at pp. 389–90.

39. 412 US 94 (1973).

40. The dissenting opinion of Justice Brennan and Marshall urged the striking of a balance:

The Court's reliance on the Fairness Doctrine as the sole means of informing the public seriously misconstrues and underestimates the public's interest in receiving ideas and information directly from the advocates of those ideas without the interposition of journalistic middlemen. . . . Our legal system reflects a belief that truth is best illuminated by a collision of genuine advocates. Under the Fairness Doctrine, however, accompanied by an absolute ban on editorial advertising, the public is compelled to rely exclusively on the "journalistic discretion" of broadcasters who serve in theory as surrogate spokesmen from all sides of all issues. This separation of the advocate from the expression of his views can serve only to diminish the effectiveness of that expression. . . . If the public is to be honestly and forthrightly apprised of opposing views on controversial issues, it is imperative that citizens be permitted at least some opportunity to speak directly for themselves as genuine advocates on issues that concern them. . . . Moreover, a proper balancing of the competing First Amendment interests at stake in this controversy must consider, not only the interests of broadcasters and of the listening and viewing public, but also the independent First Amendment interest of groups and individuals in effective self-expression. . . . The right to speak can flourish only if it is allowed to operate in an effective forum—whether it be a public park, a schoolroom, a town meeting hall, or a radio and television frequency. For in the absence of an effective means of communication, the right to speak would ring hollow indeed. . . . Any policy that absolutely denies citizens access to the airwaves necessarily renders even the concept of "full and free discussion" practically meaningless. Regretably, it is precisely such a policy that the Court upholds today. (Pp. 188–96)

41. 438 US 726 (1978).
42. 55 USLW 2175 (1987), affg 800 F2d 989 (10th Cir., 1986).
43. The Utah statute definition is as follows:

(4) "Indecent material" means a visual or verbal description display, representation, dissemination, or verbal description of: (a) a human sexual or execretory organ or function; or (b) a state of undress so as to expose the human male or female genitals, pubic area, or buttocks, with less than a fully opaque covering, or showing of the female breast with less than a fully opaque covering of any portion below the top of the nipple; or (c) an ultimate sexual act, normal or perverted, actual or simulated; or (d) masturbation, which the average person applying contemporary community standards for cable television or pay-for-viewing television programming would find is presented in a patently offensive way for the time, place, manner and context in which the material is presented. (Utah Code Ann Sec. 76-10-1702[4])

44. 611 F Supp 1099 (Utah, 1985).
45. Id.
46. See Utah Code Ann Sec. 76-10-1206 (1978), which provides in part:

Dealing in harmful material to a minor. (1) A person is guilty of dealing in harmful material when, knowing that a person is a minor, or having failed to exercise reasonable care in ascertaining the proper age of a minor, he (a) knowingly distributes or offers to distribute, exhibits or offers to exhibit, any harmful material to a minor . . . (11) "harmful to minors" means that quality of any description or representation, in whatsoever form, of nudity, sexual conduct, sexual excitement, or sadomasochistic abuse when it: (i) taken as a whole, appeals to the prurient interest in sex of minors; (ii) is patently offensive to prevailing standards in the adult community as a whole with respect to what is suitable material for minors . . . [and] (iii) taken as a whole, does not have serious value for minors. Serious value includes only serious literary, artistic, political, or scientific value for minors.

47. (Univ of Cal Press, 1987).
48. 407 US 551 (1972).
49. Id. at pp. 580–81.
50. 786 F2d 1233 (5th Cir., 1986).
51. —NY2d—, —NE2d— (Unreported, 1980).
52. See New York Times (July 11, 1987) at p. 35.
53. 447 US 74 (1980).
54. Id.

55. 444 US 164 (1975).
56. 635 P2d 108 (Wash., 1981).
57. Infra note 45.
58. Id. at p. 83.
59. See section 2.1 herein.
60. See Ely, Democracy and Distrust (1980) at pp. 73–134.
61. 260 US 393 (1922).
62. See 84 Marq L Rev 507 (1981) at p. 526.
63. Infra note 45.
64. See New York Times (April 29, 1987) at p. A28.
65. 55 USLW 4781 (1987).
66. See Pennsylvania Coal Co. v. Mahon, 260 US 393 (1922).
67. Note Andrus v. Allard, 444 US 1 (1979).

6

State Constitutions and Protection of Freedom of Speech on Private Property

Every state constitution, like the U.S. Constitution and the First Amendment, protects the freedom of expression.[1] The state protection is frequently more encompassing than the guarantees of the federal First Amendment.[2] The Wisconsin Supreme Court in McCauley v. Tropic of Cancer[3] admitted that the state may "permit greater freedom of speech" than the Fourteenth Amendment would require; and the U.S. Supreme Court in the Pruneyard case[4] applauded the California Constitution, which gave greater protection to the fundamental freedom of speech than the minimum required by the U.S. Constitution. The highest court rejected the argument that the owners of the shopping center had been unconstitutionally coerced under the California Constitution to allow the property to be used as a forum for the free speech of all citizens; the court opined that, by choice of the owners, the shopping center was open to the public and nothing prevented the owners from disclaiming any association with those citizens' giving vent to their freedom of expression.[5] It is interesting to discern that Article I, section 1, of the California Constitution did give heed to "property rights": "All people are by nature free and independent and have inalienable rights. Among these are enjoying and defending life and liberty, acquiring, possessing, and protecting property."

In Cologne v. Westfarms Associates,[6] the Connecticut Supreme Court ruled that Article 1, sections 4 and 14, of the Connecticut Constitution gives greater protection to freedom of speech and of expression than does the First Amendment.[7] Here, the plaintiffs were the National Organization of Women, and the defendants were the owners of a huge thirty-six acre shopping mall. Plaintiffs asked permission to enter the mall for the express purpose of soliciting signatures for a petition in support of the proposed equal rights amendment to the U.S. Constitution. Defendants denied this permission on the ground of its policy that barred persons "seeking signatures on petitions." The trial court granted an injunction in favor of plaintiffs to enter the private premises, subject to such restrictions as (1) on Saturdays or one alternate day during normal business hours; (2) use of a table not to exceed three feet by six feet in size and four chairs, and use of a litter receptacle; (3) posting of two signs, not to exceed two feet by three feet; (4) operation confined to center and within ten feet of table; (5) normal tone of voice without sound or radio recordings; (6) no verbal solicitation of patrons of the mall; (7) no eating or drinking at table or in surrounding area; and (8) defendants were to protect plaintiffs at all times. Interestingly, plaintiffs had made no claim under the First Amendment but had rested their case entirely on two Connecticut Constitution provisions: "Every citizen may freely speak, write and publish his sentiments on all subjects, being responsible for the abuse of that liberty" (Article 1, section 4), and, "The citizens have a right, in a peaceable manner, to assembly for their common good, and to apply to those invested with the powers of government, for redress of grievances, or other proper purposes, by petition, address, or remonstrance" (Article 1, section 14).[8] The Connecticut Supreme Court, in affirming, relied on the decision of the U.S. Supreme Court in Robins v. Pruneyard Shopping Center[9] and held that a state could grant free speech rights under its own constitution that are more expansive than those free speech rights protected under the First Amendment: "The United States Constitution . . . defines the minimum level of rights that citizens are afforded. . . . State courts, through interpretation of their constitutions, may extend the individual liberties of their citizens beyond those conferred by the federal constitution."[10] Citing its 1977 case of Horton v. Meskill,[11] in which the court upheld a finding that free public education is a fundamental right under the Connecticut, the 1982 Connecticut Supreme Court opined:

In the area of fundamental civil liberties, which includes all protections of the declaration of rights contained in Article 1 of the Connecticut Constitution, we sit as a court of last resort, subject only to the qualification that our interpretations may not restrict the guarantees accorded the national citizenry under the federal charter. In such constitutional adjudication, our first reference is Connecticut law and the full panoply of rights Connecticut residents have come to expect as their due. Accordingly, decisions of the United States Supreme Court defining fundamental rights are persuasive authority to be afforded respectful consideration, but they are to be followed by Connecticut courts only when they provide no less individual protection than is guaranteed by Connecticut law.[12]

Thus, the state constitution is an independent source of individual rights and is accorded respect only when it does not conflict with the First Amendment here.

In deciding for the plaintiffs in the Cologne case,[13] the Connecticut court found no unlawful taking in violation of the Fifth Amendment, for the activities of the plaintiffs "would not so affect the value or use of the mall . . . [and] interference with the mall's commercial functions can be minimized by the defendants' reasonable time, place and manner regulations which plaintiffs have indicated they are willing to accept."[14] Noting that Connecticut in 1973 had ratified the proposed ERA amendment, the court acknowledged the state's interest in aiding plaintiffs' in their signature solicitation activities. On the issue that the injunction denied defendants' First Amendment rights unless defendants could exclude plaintiffs from the mall for expressing views with which defendants did not necessarily agree or which defendants did not care to have expressed on their property, the court observed that defendants could expressly disavow any connection with the plaintiffs by simply posting signs to that effect. The court applauded the ruling of the Washington Supreme Court in Alderwood Associates v. Washington Environmental Council,[15] involving a shopping center of about the same size, for establishing the factors to be considered by courts in balancing the interests of property owners and individuals intent upon exercising their fundamental freedoms of speech and expression on private property: (1) the nature of the speech activity; (2) the nature and use of the property, which the Connecticut court observed here was "open to the public" and therefore "the owner has a reduced expectation of privacy, and, as a corollary, any speech activity is less threatening to the property's value";[16] and (3) the potential for reasonable regulation of the speech activity. The free speech rights under the Connecticut Constitution were not intended to be absolute, for the speaker is "responsible for the abuse of that liberty."[17] However, the speech activity is guaranteed because under section 5 of Article 1, "No law shall ever be passed to curtail or restrain the liberty of speech."

The Ninth Amendment to the U.S. Constitution, it should be noted, states that the enumeration of certain rights in it does not mean that there are not other rights that can and should be protected, as under state constitutions. Indeed, state constitutions are admittedly fertile ground for developing speech rights,[18] and apparently every state constitution, except that of Rhode Island, guarantees the right of free speech.[19] At least thirty-eight state constitutions affirmatively pronounce that freedom of speech is guaranteed,[20] and therefore it would appear that such affirmative speech provisions require less state action than would be required under the First Amendment.[21]

One Batchelder in 1982 sued the owner of a shopping center in Massachusetts that prohibited him from soliciting in the shopping center certain signatures in support of ballot access. Under the Massachusetts Constitution,[22] he was given that right to do so "in a reasonable and unobtrusive manner, in the common areas of a large shopping mall, subject to reasonable regulations adopted by the mall owner." In Batchelder v. Allied Stores

International,[23] the Massachusetts Supreme Judicial Court observed at the outset that "considerations under the Constitution of the United States appear to be substantially neutral on the issue before us," and therefore this state court addressed the issue in terms of the Massachusetts Constitution.[24] The court observed that "a majority of the State courts that have recently considered rights under State Constitutions to engage in orderly free speech, free assembly, or electoral activity on private property held open to the public, have recognized such a right. . . . A person needing signatures for ballot access requires personal contact with voters. He or she cannot reasonably obtain them in any other way. Reasonable access to the public is essential in ballot access matters."[25] The dissent, embracing the views of three of the seven justices, took the position that the Massachusetts Constitution did not apply to "private conduct of the type to which the plaintiff objects," only to "state action," which was not present here.[26]

The highest courts of Washington, New Jersey, and California have recently ruled that citizens have a right to exercise their state-given free speech rights in a reasonable manner at privately owned shopping centers and universities.[27] The Pennsylvania Supreme Court in Commonwealth of Pennsylvania v. Tate[28] reaffirmed that a state may provide through its constitution a basis for the rights and liberties of its citizens independent of that provided by the U.S. Constitution, and the rights so guaranteed may be more expansive than their federal counterparts.

In Woodland v. Michigan Citizens Lobby,[29] the Michigan Supreme Court found that the state constitution's Declaration of Rights guaranteeing rights of free expression did not prohibit owners of large private shopping malls from denying and restricting access to private individuals seeking to exercise those rights of free expression.[30] According to the court, "The Michigan Constitution's Declaration of Rights provisions have never been interpreted as extending to purely private conduct; these provisions have consistently been interpreted as limited to protection against State action."

There are many dimensions to the state's responsibility to shape its policies to comply with the priority of free speech principles under the First Amendment, such as the dispensing of information relevant to the critical moral independence of its citizens.[31] Indeed, the state has a legal obligation to ensure a rich matrix of public forums required for the exercise of free speech principles, especially since most state constitution provisions for freedom of speech are directed against private activities, as well as against government action.[32] The 1987 New York decision in Parks v. Steinbrenner[33] is an appropriate example of State action in carefully and properly defining the limits of free speech on private property. Here defendant, the principal owner of the New York Yankees baseball team, allegedly issued press releases criticizing the abilities of plaintiff as a major league umpire.[34] Plaintiff thereupon sued for defamation, and the New

York appellate court found no basis upon which liability could be predicated. The press releases are

"a constitutionally protected expression of pure opinion. In all defamation cases, the threshold issue which must be determined, as a matter of law, is whether the complained of statements constitute fact or opinion. If they fall within the ambit of 'pure opinion,' then even if false and libelous, and no matter how pejorative or pernicious they may be, such statements are safeguarded and may not serve as the basis for an action in defamation."[35]

The New York court concluded:

The reverence which the First Amendment accords to ideas has properly resulted in the determination that, "however pernicious an opinion may seem, we depend for its correction not on the conscience of judges and juries but on the competition of other ideas." (*Gertz v. Robert Welch, Inc.*, 418 US 323, 339–340.) Those competing ideas about baseball's arbiters will undoubtedly continue to abound aplenty both on the playing fields and in the sports columns, albeit not in the courtroom.

NOTES

1. See generally 20 Stan L Rev 318 (1968) and 4 Vand L Rev 620 (1951).
2. Cf. Freedman v. State, 197 A2d 232 (Md., 1984), revd 350 US 51 (1965).
3. 121 NW2d 545 (Wisc., 1963).
4. 447 US 17 (1980).
5. See 18 Am Bus L J 562 (1981) at p. 566.
6. 442 A2d 471 (Conn., 1982).
7. See 56 Conn Bar J (1982) at pp. 305 et seq.
8. See section 2.6 herein.
9. 447 US 17 (1980).
10. Infra note 6 at p. 477.
11. 376 A2d 359 (Conn., 1977).
12. Id.
13. Infra note 6.
14. Infra note 6 at p. 483.
15. 635 P2d 108 (Wash., 1981).
16. Infra note 6 at p. 482.
17. Article 1, section 4 of the Connecticut Constitution.
18. See generally 90 Harv L Rev 489 (1977) and 45 U Cin L Rev 1 (1976).
19. RI Const, Art I, section 19, expressly guarantees freedom of the press but not freedom of speech.
20. Ala Const Art I, sec 4; Alas Const Art I, sec 5; Ariz Const Art II; Ark Const Art 2, sec 6; Cal Const Art I, sec 2(a); Colo Const Art II, sec 10; Conn Const Art 1, sec 4; Fla Const Art I, sec 4; Ga Const Art I, sec 1, par IV; Idaho Const Art I, sec 1; Iowa Consnt Art I, sec 7; Kan Const Bill of Rts, sec 11; Ky Const Bill of Rts, sec 8; La Const Art I, sec 7; Maine Const Art I, sec 3; Md Const

Decl of Rts, Art 40; Mich Const Art I, sec 5; Minn Const Art I, sec 3; Miss Const Art 3, sec 11; Mo Const Art I, sec 8; Mont Const Art II, sec 7; Nebr Const Art I, sec 5; Nev Const Art I, sec 9; NJ Const Art I, par 6; NM Const Art II, sec 17; NY Const, Art I, sec 8; ND Const Art I, sec 4; Ohio Const Art I, sec 11; Okla Const Art II, sec 22; Pa Const Art I, sec 7; SD Const Art VI, sec 5; Tenn Const Art I, sec 19; Tex Const Art I, sec 8; Va Const Art I, sec 12; Wash Const Art I, sec 5; Wis Const Art I, sec 3; Wyo Const Art I, sec 20.

21. According to 37 Syracuse L Rev 1 (1986) at p. 22, footnote 140, there are forty-four states whose free speech provision does not require state action. Only Hawaii, Indiana, Oregon, South Carolina, Utah, and West Virginia appear to have express state action requisites.

22. Articles 9 and 16 of the Declaration of Rights.

23. 445 NE2d 590 (Mass., 1983).

24.

Free from any demonstrated restraint or mandate under the Constitution of the United States, we address Batchelder's arguments based on the Declaration of Rights of the Constitution of the Commonwealth. He relies both on the freedom of speech provisions of Article 16 of the Declaration of Rights, as amended by Article 77 of the Amendments to the Massachusetts Constitution ("The right of free speech shall not be abridged"), and on Article 9, concerning the freedom and equality of elections. We need not consider Batchelder's arguments under Article 16, in view of our interpretation of Article 9. Unlike the prohibition of the First Amendment to the Federal Constitution . . . Article is not by its terms directed only against governmental action. There is, thus, no "State action" requirement expressed in Article 9, and we see no reason to imply such a requirement, and thereby to force a parallelism with the Federal Constitution. Courts in other States have regarded as meaningful the absence of State action language in their State constitutions. . . . We think that the distinction is significant and reject any suggestion that the Declaration of Rights should be read as directed exclusively toward restraining government action.

25. Id. at p. 595.

26. See section 4.1 herein. The dissenting opinion argued that "history and logic persuade me that our State Constitution should be read as incorporating a threshold requirement of State action before the courts may act to protect asserted rights under the Declaration of Rights. Furthermore, I see no reason to find Article 9 a guarantee of greater rights than those protected under the Federal Constitution. . . . I would hold . . . that [plaintiff] had no further right, under the State Constitution, to carry his efforts into the North Shore shopping center."

27. See Alderwood Associates v. Washington Environmental Council, 635 P2d 108 (Wash., 1981), inter alia.

28. 432 A2d 1382 (Pa., 1981).

29. 378 NW2d 337 (Mich., 1985).

30. "That the state constitution may afford greater protections than the federal constitution is also well established and is based on fundamental constitutional doctrine and principles of federalism. . . . The Michigan Constitution has been interpreted as affording broader protection of some individual rights also guaranteed by the federal constitution's Bill of Rights."

31. See Richmond Newspapers, Inc. v. Virginia, 448 US 555 (1980).

32. Infra note 22.

33. —AD2d—, —NYS2d— (1st Dep., July 23, 1987).

34. The press releases stated:

"Judging off his last two days' performance, my people tell me that he is not a capable umpire. He is a member of one of the finest crews umpiring in the American League today, but obviously he doesn't measure up.

"We are making no excuse for the team's play this season, but this weekend our team has had several key injuries and for umpire Dallas Parks to throw two of our players out of ballgames in two days on plays he misjudges is ludicrous.

"This man, in my opinion, has had it in for the Yankees ever since I labeled him and several of the umpires as 'scabs' because they worked the American League's games in 1979 during the umpires' strike.

"Parks must learn that the word scab is a commonly-used phrase. It is in no way meant as a personal insult. However, because he worked during the strike for baseball management does not mean he should be protected by them and annually given a job he is not capable of handling."

35. The thrust of the opinion is seen in the following paragraphs:

A brief historical perspective indicates that there are indeed such relevant customs and conventions. While it was an honor to be selected as the esteemed umpire in the early days of baseball, when it was known as a "gentleman's sport," that position changed markedly with the growth of professionalism in the 1870's, when the position of the umpire concomitantly declined and a lengthy history of abuse took hold. Albert G. Spalding, one of the pioneering promoters of the game, is reported to have said that by harassing umpires, fans were exercising their democratic right to oppose tyrants. Baltimore manager Ned Hanlon, one of the leading strategists of the 1890s's, observed that "it is impossible to prevent expressions of impatience or actions indicating dissent with the umpire's decision" and advised umpires to accept abuse as part of their rule. From the late nineteenth century on, the baseball umpire has come to expect not only verbal abuse, but in many cases, physical attack as well, as part of the "robust debate" ingrained in the profession.

Despite claims by umpires, such as the legendary Bill Klem, that they "never called one wrong," fans continue to exercise their right to vent their spleen on the men in blue. In 1940 one fan jumped out of the stands at Ebbets Field to "flatten" umpire George Magerkurth with his fists. When the fan's photograph appeared in the newspaper the next day, it was learned that he risked more than the exercise of his "right to question the umpire"—the attacker was a paroled felon who was promptly returned to jail for violating his parole. Yet Magerkurth, perhaps in deference to this deep-rooted tradition of dissent, never pressed charges for the assault. As recently as the 1985 World Series, many reacted with glee, rather than horror, when Pitcher Joaquin Andujar attacked umpire Don Denkinger on the field of play. This long-standing tradition may explain why General Douglas MacArthur is reported to have said on his return to American soil that he was proud to protect American freedoms, like the freedom to boo the umpire.

Judges, too, have expressed their acceptance of this American tradition. In dismissing a minor league general manager's defamation action on other grounds, the U.S. District Court noted the history of the exchange of harsh insults, especially those with an umpire, which has gained commonplace acceptance in the world of baseball. (*King v. Burris*, 588 F. Supp 1152, 1157). In a personal injury action arising from a softball game, this court took occasion to characterize the umpire as "proverbially a dominating and inflexible figure." (*Forkash v. City of New York*, 27 AD 2d 831, 832). The contemporary view of a baseball umpire was perhaps best summed up by the Supreme Court of North Carolina in an action brought by a minor league umpire charging a team with failing to provide adequate safety and police protection from a fan who physically assaulted him. (*Toone v. Adams*, 262 NC 403, 137 SE 2d, 132, 136, 10 ALR 3d 435.) The court here aptly stated:

"For present day fans, a goodly part of the sport in a baseball game is goading and denouncing the umpire when they do not concur in his decisions, and most feel that, without one or more rhubarbs, they have not received their money's worth. Ordinarily, however, an umpire garners only vituperation—not fisticuffs. Fortified by the knowledge of his infallibility in all judgment decisions, he is able to shed billingsgate like water on the proverbial duck's back."

When Steinbrenner's remarks are viewed in this context, it is clear that they would be perceived by the average reader as a statement of opinion, and not fact.

Commercial Speech and Its Protection Under the First Amendment

7.1 UNPROTECTED COMMERCIAL SPEECH

Historically, the right of free speech was applied only to speech that transmitted political or social ideas, not to speech that concerned commerce or commercial advertising. Commercial speech may be questionably distinguished from noncommercial speech on the basis of information function, subject matter, economic motivation, and contractual nature.[1] It was not until the year 1942 that commercial speech was urged for First Amendment protection; but the U.S. Supreme Court in Valentine v. Chrestensen[2] then rejected First Amendment protection for commercial speech. Here the Court considered a First Amendment challenge to a municipal ordinance that prohibited the distribution of commercial handbills. One side of the commercial handbill featured an advertisement for a submarine exhibit, and the other side contained a written protest against the municipality's refusal to provide a pier for the exhibit. Although the Court recognized that the handbill contained both a commercial and a noncommercial message, it ruled that the handbill was still not protected by the First Amendment. Undoubtedly the Court reasoned that the economic motive to advertise may have provided a consistent and powerful motive for commercial speech that would counterbalance any adverse effect from governmental prohibition of such advertising, and therefore protection under the First Amendment was deemed unnecessary. The Court opined that the First Amendment "imposes no such restraint on government as respects purely commercial advertising."[3]

There are reasons why prohibitions on commercial speech and commercial advertising might not always implicate the values of free speech or expression. First, advertising generally does not state opinions or values central to those views and opinions on social, political, and economic matters that are usually protected by free speech; second, the communicative contexts of commercial speech and commercial advertising do not lend themselves to the usual free speech presumption that dangerous speech may be rebutted in the normal course of interchange of ideas and opinions. Implicit in these two reasons is the acknowledgment that commercial speech neither expresses nor appeals to moral powers. But the argument against First Amendment protection for commercial speech and commercial advertising simply does not hold water. Persons express their moral powers of rationality and reasonableness in many ways, including commercial product advertising and other forms of commercial speech. Also, since free speech protects the communicative integrity not only of speakers but of audiences as well, commercial speech can also perform that function. Advertising sets forth information about cheaper and better products and services that may enable a person to define and pursue personal and moral aims.[4]

The 1942 pronouncement of the U.S. Supreme Court in the Valentine case[5] meant that commercial speech was inferior to speech that related to economic, political, or social information. Commercial speech was treated as a form of expression relating to property rights and regulated like any other economic opportunity.[6] It was placed in the unprotected category, such as child pornography,[7] defamation or libel,[8] obscenities,[9] and insults, as delineated in Chaplinsky v. New Hampshire,[10] where the highest court observed that insulting or "fighting" words "have never been thought to raise any Constitutional problem . . . such utterances are no essential part of any exposition of ideas, and are of such slight social value as a step to truth that any benefit that may be derived from them is clearly outweighed by the social interest in order and morality."[11] But such unprotected speech might still not pass constitutional muster if it involves "prior restraint;" and in that event, at least three procedural prerequisites must be met if such unprotected speech is to obviate "the dangers of censorship systems." "First, the burden of instituting judicial proceedings, and of proving that the material is unprotected, must rest on the censor. Second, any restraint prior to judicial review can be imposed only for a specified brief period and only for the purpose of preserving the status quo. Third, a prompt final judicial determination must be assured."[12]

The U.S. Supreme Court in 1943 in Martin v. City of Struthers[13] protected the right of a Jehovah's Witness to distribute door to door handbills advertising religious meetings under the guise that defendant was disseminating ideas. But eight years later, in Breard v. Alexandria,[14] the Court denied First Amendment protection to communications of a door-to-door brush salesman on the ground that his utterances were of economic origin and made for profit, that is, commercial speech. In 1964, the landmark case of New York Times Co. v. Sullivan[15] prompted the highest court to recognize that some advertisements were not purely commercial speech.

Here an elected public official from Alabama brought a libel action against four clergymen and the *New York Times* because of an advertisement in the newspaper that included statements about police activity directed toward members of the civil rights movement. Plaintiff contended that the First Amendment was not applicable since the libel was published as part of a paid commercial advertisement. But the Court rejected that argument, holding that the newspaper advertisement "communicated information, expressed opinion, recited grievances, protested claimed abuses, and sought financial support on behalf of a movement whose existence and objectives are matters of the highest public interest and concern."[16] The fact that the *New York Times* received payment for the advertisement was immaterial, according to the Court.

In Sniadach v. Family Finance Corp.[17] and in Goldberg v. Kelly,[18] the U.S. Supreme Court in 1969 and 1970, respectively, viewed "economic rights" in as favorable a light as it had viewed "political rights," and the Court commenced to protect "economic rights," particularly of the poor. In 1973 in Pittsburgh Press Co. v. Pittsburgh Commission on Human Relations,[19] the Court opined that the newspaper's decision "to accept a commercial advertisement which the advertiser directs to be placed in a sex designated column . . . lifts the newspaper's actions from the category of commercial speech." But the Court labeled the advertisements as "classic examples of commercial speech" unprotected by the First Amendment: "Any First Amendment interest which might be served by advertising an ordinary commercial proposal and might arguably outweigh the governmental interest supporting the regulation is altogether absent when the commercial activity itself is illegal and the restriction on advertising is incidental to a valid limitation on economic activity."[20]

In 1975 in Bigelow v. Commonwealth of Virginia,[21] the U.S. Supreme Court recognized the error of its ways and for the first time accorded commercial speech the protection of the First Amendment. Here, editor Bigelow was convicted under a Virginia statute that made the circulation of any publication to "encourage or promote processing of an abortion" a misdemeanor; he had communicated in the advertisement the fact that abortions were legal in New York and that services of a referral agency were offered.[22] The Virginia Supreme Court regarded the advertisement as paid commercial speech not entitled to First Amendment protection, but the U.S. Supreme Court reversed, holding that speech does not lose its constitutional protection merely because it appears as an advertisement. First Amendment protection is afforded where the speech does more than simply propose a commercial transaction, where it contains factual material of clear public interest, and where portions constitute an exercise of the freedom to communicate information and disseminate opinion: "Regardless of the particular label . . . whether it [the commonwealth of Virginia] calls speech 'commercial' or 'commercial' advertising or 'solicitation'—a court may not escape the task of assessing the First Amendment interest at stake and weighing it against the public interest allegedly served by the regulation. The diverse motives, means, and messages of advertising may make speech 'commercial' in widely varying degrees."[23] The Court opined that "the relationship of speech to the marketplace of products or services does not make it valueless in the marketplace of ideas."[24] Obviously the advertisement, while proposing a commercial transaction, was more preoccupied with the exercise of free speech regarding the controversial issue of abortion.

The next year, in Virginia State Board of Pharmacy v. Virginia Citizens Consumer Council,[25] the highest court characterized this case as one in which "the notion of 'unprotected commercial speech' all but passed from the scene."[26] Here a consumer group challenged a Virginia statute that declared it unprofessional for a licensed pharmacist to advertise the prices of prescription drug products. The U.S. Supreme Court took the occasion to give unqualified blessing and protection under the First Amendment to commercial speech: "Advertising, however tasteless and excessive it may seem, is nonetheless dissemination of information as to who is producing and selling what product, for what reason, and at what price. So long as we preserve a predominantly free enterprise economy, the allocation of our resources in large measure will be made through numerous private economic decisions. It is a matter of public interest that those decisions, in the aggregate, be intelligent and well informed. To this end, the free flow of commercial information is indispensable."[27] However, the Court was unwilling to extend absolute protection to commercial speech or any other form of social or economic speech, as it stressed that some regulation as to time, place, and manner is permissible to ensure that commercial and other speech flow "cleanly as well as freely."[28] Commercial speech, according to the Court, possesses certain characteristics that render it amenable to reasonable regulation, for example, it is readily verifiable—and the profit motive behind the expression largely prevents "chilling" by governmental regulation.[29]

The following year of 1977 brought Linmark Associates v. Township of Willingboro.[30] The Court here struck down a ban on the use of "for sale" or "sold" signs where the purpose was to stem the flight of white home owners from a racially integrated residential community. First Amendment protection was also given to advertising in connection with legal services[31] and the sale and distribution of contraceptives to persons under sixteen years of age[32] but not to advertising the practice of optometry without a trade name (because the Court was convinced that such practice was likely to mislead consumers).[33] In another case, an attorney offered by letter free representation to a person who had been sterilized as a condition of continued medical assistance. The Court held that her speech was protected as a part of associational activity and expression intended to convey ideas and beliefs.[34]

In the 1978 decision in First National Bank of Boston v. Bellotti[35] the highest court struck down a state ban on corporate commercial advocacy and proclaimed that the First Amendment protects speech, whether or not it protects the particular speaker.[36] Corporate commercial speech does not lose its protected character because of its corporate character. Here was a bold attempt to silence corporate opposition to a proposed Massachusetts constitutional amendment authorizing the legislature to impose a graduated tax on the income of individuals. The Massachusetts law forbade a corporation to expend funds to communicate its views about any referendum subject that did not materially affect the corporate business.[37] The Court found that Massachusetts was "dictating the subjects about which persons may speak and the speakers who may address a public issue."[38] The 5–4 majority opinion pointed out that "the inherent worth of the speech in terms of its capacity for informing the public does not depend upon the identity of its source, whether corporation, association, union or individual."[39]

The 1980 decision of the U.S. Supreme Court in Central Hudson Gas & Electric Co. v. Public Service Commission,[40] which struck down on First Amendment grounds a prohibition on promotional advertising of electricity by public utilities, set forth a detailed four-part test of governmental regulation of commercial speech.[41] The New York trial court had held that the ban on promotional advertising by the Public Service Commission (PSC) was justified by the compelling state interest in energy conservation.[42] The New York Court of Appeals affirmed on the ground that commercial speech was entitled to less constitutional protection, especially since the disseminator of the information was in a noncompetitive industry in which the data could only marginally affect the accuracy of private economic decision making.[43] The four-part test of governmental regulation of commercial speech, as set forth by the U.S. Supreme Court, was derived from the Court's conviction that the protection to be afforded any particular commercial message should turn on both the nature of the expression and the strength of the governmental interests served by the restriction.[44] Within this framework, a Court must determine (1) if the commercial message is more likely to deceive than accurately to inform the public or if it promotes unlawful activity, in which event such commercial speech is unprotected by the First Amendment; (2) if the state proffers a substantial governmental interest to sustain the content-based restriction, then protection may not result; (3) if the restriction does not ineffectually or remotely support but "directly advances" the asserted interest, then protection may not result; and (4) "if the governmental interest could be served as well by a more limited restriction on commercial speech, the excessive restrictions cannot survive."[45] Applying this four-part test, the Court declared that the ban on promotional advertising violated the First Amendment. The PSC regulation was not designed to achieve asserted state interests in energy conservation or distributional fairness in electricity rates.[46]

The concurring opinion of Justice Blackmun demonstrated that the "regulatory measure struck at the heart of the First Amendment" in that it entailed "a convert attempt by the State to manipulate the choices of its citizens . . . by depriving the public of information needed to make a free choice."[47] The sole dissent, by Justice Rehnquist, found the majority's analysis to be overprotective of commercial speech and "virtually indistinguishable" from noncommercial expression. He opined that the "substantial State interest" should override the concern for a "free flow of information."[48]

Thus, protection was afforded under the First Amendment to commercial speech, defined in the Central Hudson case[49] as "expression related solely to the economic interests of the speaker and its audience." But it is submitted that this result is buttressed by the realization that such speech has never been distinguished satisfactorily from noncommercial expression.[50] Indeed, no commercial speech is entirely devoid of noncommercial speech, with perhaps political, economic, or social overtones. And a state should not be permitted to control commercial speech as an incident to its control over the economic operations of the speaker.[51] In 1981 in In Re R.M.J.,[52] Justice Powell had occasion to discuss the boundaries of commercial speech regulation with respect to lawyer advertising: "Truthful advertising related to lawful activities is entitled to the protections of the First Amendment. But when the particular content of method of advertising suggests that it is inherently misleading or when experience has provided that in fact such advertising is subject to abuse, the States may impose appropriate (and reasonably necessary) restrictions. . . . But the State must assert a substantial interest and the interference with speech must be in proportion to the interest served."[53]

Four years later, in Zauderer v. Office of Disciplinary Counsel of the Supreme Court of Ohio,[54] the highest court loosened the restrictions on lawyer advertising by holding that the state prohibition on self-recommendations in lawyer advertising violated the First Amendment:[55] "Our recent decisions involving commercial speech have been grounded in the faith that the free flow of commercial information is valuable enough to justify imposing on would-be-regulators the costs of distinguishing the truthful from the false, the helpful from the misleading, and the harmless from the harmful."[56] And in Lowe v. Securities Exchange Commission,[57] where the U.S. Supreme Court granted certiorari to consider the constitutional question of whether an injunction against Lowe's publication and distribution of newsletters was prohibited by the First Amendment, the Court simply found the ban to be too broad to survive even the lesser scrutiny of commercial speech.[58] Justice White opined that the act was "too blunt an in-strument to survive even the reduced level of scrutiny called for by the restrictions on commercial speech."[59] The newsletters clearly proposed commercial transactions related to the speaker's economic interests, al-though the speaker did not sell the proposed stock. Protection of such commercial speech belongs within the parameters of the First Amend-ment. The dissent of Justice Douglas in Dun & Bradstreet, Inc. v. Grave[60] is worth noting: "The language of the First Amendment does not except speech directed at private economic decision-making. Certainly such speech could not be regarded as less important than political expression."

In 1986 in Posadas de Puerto Rico Associates v. Tourism Company of Puerto Rico,[61] the highest court upheld a Puerto Rican law that forbade advertisements inviting citizens of Puerto Rico to gamble legally in casi-nos. The apparent discrimination between citizens of Puerto Rico and non-citizens of Puerto Rico was obvious; furthermore, Puerto Rico had a sub-stantial interest in reducing the demand for casino gambling among its citizens because excessive gambling "would produce serious harmful ef-fects on the health, safety and welfare of Puerto Rican citizens, such as the . . . increase in local crime, the fostering of prostitution . . . and the infiltration of organized crime."[62] Chief Justice Rehnquist found that the exclusion of other forms of gambling such as horse racing, cock-fighting, and the State-run lottery was reasonable because those forms of gambling had a longer tradition in Puerto Rico and posed a less serious threat. Also, the fact that Puerto Rico chose to make casino gambling illegal meant that Puerto Rico could exercise the power of forbidding "the stimulation of demand for casino gambling through advertising."[63] The dissenting opin-ion of Justice Brennan attacked the majority opinion for speculating about what reasons might have motivated the Puerto Rican legislature to ban advertisements rather than waiting for Puerto Rico to prove which inter-ests it sought to promote and how substantial it considered those inter-ests.[64] That dissent also pointed out that the majority of the 5–4 court ignored alternative means of achieving the government's goal that would not have intruded on First Amendment values. The dissent of Justice Ste-vens concentrated on the issue of discrimination.[65] All nine justices "aban-doned the Central Hudson case.[66] compromise and retreated toward polar ideals of complete individual autonomy and uninhibited government con-trol."[67]

7.2 COMMERCIAL SPEECH IN ACTION

The four-part test for commercial speech protection under the First Amendment, as set forth in the Central Hudson case,[68] has produced in-teresting examples of commercial speech in action. Before governmental regulation of commercial speech is approved, the commercial speech must be illegal or misleading (test 1); there must be a substantial government interest (test 2); the regulation must directly advance the governmental interest (test 3); and the regulation must be no more extensive than necessary to further the governmental interest (test 4).

Test 1 is illustrated by Pittsburgh Press Co. v. Human Relations Commission,[69] where the highest court upheld a law prohibiting a newspaper from separating help-wanted advertisements by sex. In Hoffman Estate v. Flipside,[70] the Court upheld regulation of sales of drug paraphernalia, pointing out that the state may ban commercial activity promoting or encouraging illegal drug use.

Test 2, mandating a substantial governmental interest, may include protecting the privacy of the home,[71] the orderly movement of crowds of people,[72] the conservation of energy, even the prevention of disruption of the public school system.

Test 3 is evidenced in O'Brien v. United States,[73] where all free speech activity within fifteen feet of an escalator was prohibited in order to expedite the orderly flow of pedestrian traffic. Governmental regulation was also upheld in Rieke v. City of Overland Park[74] but narrowly construed in the regulation of searchlights, which advances traffic safety, aesthetics, and the preservation of property values.

Test 4 requires tailoring of the regulation to fit the governmental interest, as more particularly described in State of Hawaii v. Bloss.[75] Here the Hawaiian statute failed the test because the prohibition on free speech was absolute and was more extensive than necessary to further the governmental interest.[76] In First National Bank of Boston v. Bellotti,[77] the U.S. Supreme Court had found that the governmental criminal statute was not necessary to preserve "the State's interest in sustaining the active role of the individual citizen in the electoral process." Yet the Court had ruled that corporate speech could be regulated in the interest of preventing corporate speech from drowning out individual speech. Here the Court had overturned a Massachusetts criminal statute forbidding banks and business corporations from making expenditures intended to influence referenda concerning issues not "materially affecting" their property, business, or assests. The Court opined that the more speech and information that is in circulation, the better off society is and the better is the First Amendment served.[78] Indeed, according to the Court, the First Amendment "prohibits government from limiting the stock of information from which members of the public may draw."[79]

The expansion on the recognized protection of commercial speech is seen in Consumers Union of the United States, Inc. v. General Signal Corp.,[80] where the Second U.S. Court of Appeals in 1983 upheld the fair use defense to a copyright infringement. The Court permitted the manufacturer to quote from a copyrighted article in television advertisements for its product. The Fifth U.S. Court of Appeals in Herceg v. Hustler

Magazine[81] reversed a lower court verdict that gave the estate of a four-teen-year old boy $69,000 compensatory damages and $100,000 exemplary damages against the magazine publisher. In an August 1981 article, "Orgasm of Death," the writer had described masturbation while hanging oneself so as temporarily to cut off the blood supply to the brain at the moment of orgasm. An editor's note above the article urged readers not to attempt the method and warned readers at least ten times that auto-erotic asphyxiation is deadly. Nevertheless, the young teenager hanged himself. The federal district court in Texas dismissed the suit on the ground that the First Amendment barred suit except for "incitement claims." The amended complaint was dismissed also, as the federal appellate court opined: "Even if the article paints in glowing terms the pleasure supposedly achieved by the practice it describes, as the plaintiffs contend, no fair reading of it can make its content advocacy, let alone incitement to engage in the process." Previously the court had listed "incitement to imminent lawless activity" as one activity the First Amendment does not protect. The dissenting opinion of Judge Edith H. Jones stressed her belief that the majority opinion "appears to foreclose the possibility that any State might choose to temper the excesses of the pornography business by imposing civil liability for harms it directly causes."[82]

On the lighter side is Frank v. National Broadcasting Co.,[83] where the New York Appellate Division in September 1986 refused to curb the defendant's freedom of expression during a late night comedy program, "Saturday Night Live," telecast over NBC. Plaintiff (a tax consultant and accountant) was described as a tax consultant and accountant in a skit with the following monologue:

Thank you. Hello. Look at your calendar. It's April 14th. Your taxes are due tomorrow. You could wind up with your assets in a sling. So listen closely. Here are some write-offs you probably aren't familiar with—courtesy of "Fast Frank." Got a houseplant? A Ficus, a Coleus, a Boston Fern—doesn't matter. If you love it and take care of it—claim it as a dependent.

Got a horrible acne? . . . use a lotta Clearasil . . . that's an Oil-Depletion Allowance. You say your wife won't sleep with you? You got withholding tax coming back. If she walks out on you—you *lose* a dependent. *But* . . . it's a home improvement—write it off.

Should you happen, while filling out your tax form, to get a paper cut—thank your lucky stars—that's a medical expense *and* a disability. Got a rotten tomato in your fridge? Frost ruined your crops—that's a farm loss. Your tree gets Dutch Elm Disease . . . Sick leave—take a deduction. Did you take a trip to the bathroom tonight? If you *took* a trip . . . and you did *business*—you can write if off. Wait, there's more. Did you cry at "Terms of Endearment?" That's a *moving* expense. A urologist who's married to another urologist can file a joint return.

Got a piece of popcorn stuck between your teeth? . . . Or a sister who drools on her shoes? . . . You got money comin' back—and I can get it for you *fast,* because I'm Fast Frank. Call me. I have hundreds of trained relatives waiting to take your call. At Fast Frank's we guarantee your *refund* will be greater than what you *earned*.

The court ruled that there was no violation of sections 50 and 51 of the New York Civil Rights Law in that plaintiff's name was not used without permission for advertising or trade purposes, and there was no defamation as a matter of law, for the lunacy statements presented as a small comic part of a comic entertainment program were not malicious or a vicious personal attack upon the plaintiff: "It is the principal duty of the courts to reconcile the individual's interest in guarding his good name with cherished First Amendment considerations. . . . In some instances, the protection of the First Amendment approaches the absolute; for example, the expression of one's opinion, no matter how pernicious, distasteful or unpopular it may be, is not actionable." As stated in Polygram Records v. Superior Court,[84] "To hold otherwise would run afoul of the First Amendment and chill the free speech rights of all comedy performers and humorists, to the genuine detriment of our society."

Another aspect of the issue of commercial speech is seen in the recognition that the First Amendment protects not only the right to speak but also the right to refrain from speaking.[85] This concept of "negative free speech" is illustrated in Miami Herald Publishing Co. v. Tornillo,[86] where the U.S. Supreme Court struck down a Florida statute requiring newspapers to provide a right of reply to candidates whose character or record they had challenged. In Pacific Gas & Electric Co. v. Public Utilities Commission of California,[87] that right to refrain from speaking was extended to spreading another's message; the granting of access by a consumer group to the utility's billing envelopes was held to be an impermissible restriction on the utility's right of free speech. Justice Marshall, in his concurring opinion, distinguished the case from the Pruneyard Shopping Center case[88] in which the court upheld a State-granted right of access for students to distribute leaflets at a private shopping center; he argued that access in the instant case would intrude upon property that was never opened to the public and would therefore inevitably curtail the utility's freedom of speech.

NOTES

1. See generally 74 Nw U L Rev 372 (1979), and also 5 Haw L Rev 79 (1983).
2. 316 US 52 (1942).
The court contrasted advertising with protected types of communication:

This court has unequivocally held that the streets are proper places for the exercise of the freedom of communicating information and disseminating opinion and that, though the states and municipalities may appropriately regulate the privilege in the public interest, they may not unduly burden or proscribe its employment in these public thoroughfares. We are equally clear that the Constitution imposes no such restraint on government as respects purely commercial advertising. Whether, and to what extent, one may promote or pursue a gainful occupation in the streets, to what extent such activity shall be adjudged a derogation of the public right of user, are matters for legislative judgment.

The political protest did not protect the advertising on the other side of the hand-bill, as the court concluded that it was sufficient that the protest was affixed

with the intent, and for the purpose, of evading the prohibition of the ordinance. If that evasion were successful every merchant who desires to broadcast advertising leaflets in the streets need only append a civil appeal, or moral platitude, to achieve immunity from the law's command.

3. Id at p. 54.

4. See United States v. Ballard, 322 US 78 (1944).

5. Infra note 2.

6. See 17 Conn L Rev 835 (1985); also note 12 Cap U L Rev 115 (1982) and 39 Geo Wash L Rev 429 (1971).

7. See Chapter 10 to this book. Note New York v. Ferber, 458 US 747 (1982).

8. See Gertz v. Robert Welch, Inc. 418 US 323 (1974).

9. See Roth v. United States, 354 US 479 (1957).

10. 315 US 568 (1942).

11. Id. at pp. 571-72.

12. See Southeastern Promotions, Ltd. v. Conrad, 420 US 546 (1975) at p. 560. See also 90 Dick L. Rev 705 (1986).

13. 319 US 141 (1943).

14. 341 US 622 (1951).

15. 376 US 254 (1964).

16. Id. at p. 266. Note Zauderer v. Office of Disciplinary Counsel. 105 S Ct 2265 (1985) at 2277, where the U.S. Supreme Court struck down disciplinary rules for lawyers from Ohio's Code of Professional Responsibility, which forbade lawyers to use illustrations or to give advice in newspaper advertisements. Such advertisements were "conducive to reflection and the exercise of choice" and therefore were protected under the First Amendment. See generally 100 Harv L Rev 100 (1986) at p. 172.

Also note Virginia State Board of Pharmacy v. Virginia Citizens Consumer Council, Inc., 425 US 748 (1976), where the highest court rejected a "highly paternalistic approach" toward commercial speech on the assumption that "this information is not in itself harmful, that people will perceive their own best interest if only they are well enough informed, and that the best means to that end is to open the channels of communication rather than to close them."

The other side of the coin, i.e., limitation on First Amendment protection in order to uphold reasonable State regulations that protect consumers from harmful commercial speech, is seen in Friedman v. Rogers, 440 US 1 (1979) and in Ohralik v. Ohio State Bar Assn., 436 US 447 (1978).

17. 395 US 337 (1969).

18. 397 US 254 (1970).

19. 413 US 376 (1973).

20. Id. at p. 389.

21. 421 US 809 (1975).

22. The ad read:

UNWANTED PREGNANCY LET US HELP YOU. Abortions are now legal in New York. There are no residency requirements. FOR IMMEDIATE PLACEMENT IN AC-CREDITED HOSPITALS AND CLINICS AT LOW COST contact WOMEN'S PAVILION 515 Madison Avenue, New York, N.Y. 10022 or call any time (212) 371-6670 or (212) 371-6650 AVAILABLE SEVEN DAYS A WEEK STRICTLY CONFIDENTIAL. We will make all arrangements for you and help you with information and counseling.

23. Infra note 21 at p. 826.
24. Id.
25. 425 US 748 (1976).
26. Id. at p. 759.
27. Id at p. 765.
28. Id at p. 772.
29. Id.
30. 432 US 85 (1977).
31. Bates v. State Bar of Arizona, 443 US 350 (1977).
32. Carey v. Population Services International, 431 US 678 (1977).
33. See Friedman v. Rogers, 440 US 1 (1978):

A trade name that has acquired such associations to the extent of establishing a secondary meaning becomes a valuable property of the business. . . . But a property interest in a means of communication does not enlarge or diminish the First Amendment protection . . . requiring a State to allow deceptive or misleading commercial speech whenever the publi-cation of additional information can clarify or offset the effects of the spurious communica-tion.(p. 12)

34. In Re Primus, 436 US 412 (1978).
35. 98 S Ct 1407 (1978).
36. See Lamont V. Postmaster General, 381 US 301 (1965), and also Stanley v. Georgia, 394 US 557 (1969).
37. See generally Tribe, American Constitutional Law (1978) at chap. 12.
38. Infra note 35 at p. 1420.
39. Id. at p. 1421.
40. 447 US 557, 100 S Ct 2343 (1980).
41. See 94 Harv L Rev 75 (1980) at pp. 159 et seq.
42. Consolidated Edison Co. v. PSC, 407 NYS2d 735 (1978).
43. 390 NE2d 749 (N.Y., 1979).
44. Infra note 40 at p. 564 and p. 2350.
45. Id.
46. Id. at p. 567 and p. 2353-54.
47. Id. at p. 568 and p. 2355.
48. Id. at p. 578 and p. 2365.
49. Infra note 40.
50. Infra note 41 at p. 166.
51. See 65 Va L Rev 1 (1979).
52. 455 US 191 (1981).
53. Id. at p. 203.
54. 105 S Ct 2265 (1985).
55. Id. at pp. 2279-80.

56. The court did, however, uphold the defendant's position on disclosure requirements:

We do not suggest that disclosure requirements do not implicate the advertiser's First Amendment rights. . . . We recognize that unjustified or unduly burdensome disclosure requirements might offend the First Amendment by chilling protected commercial speech. But we hold that an advertiser's rights are adequately protected as long as disclosure requirements are reasonably related to the State's interest in preventing deception of consumers. (P. 2282)

57. 105 S Ct 2315 (1985).
58. See 90 Dick L Rev 705 (1986) at p. 722.
59. Infra note 57.
60. 404 US 898 (1971) at p. 905.
61. 106 S Ct 2968 (1986).
62. Id at 2977.
63. Id at 2979.
64. Id at 2984.
65. Id at 2986–87.
66. Infra note 40.
67. See 100 Harv L Rev 100 (1986) at 177.
68. Infra note 49.
69. 413 US 376 (1973).
70. 455 US 489 (1982).
71. See Carey v. Brown, 447 US 455 (1980).
72. See Heffron v. International Society for Krishna-Consciousness, 452 US 640 (1981).
73. 444 A2d 946 (DC App., 1982).
74. 657 P2d 1121 (Kan., 1983).
75. 637 P2d 1117 (Haw., 1981).
76. The vagueness of the ordinance also violated due process of law.
77. 435 US 765 (1978).
78. See generally 59 S Cal L Rev 1227 (1986).
79. Infra note 77 at p. 783.
80. 724 F2d 1044 (2d Cir., 1983), cert den 105 S Ct 100 (1984).
81. —F2d—(5th Cir., May 10, 1987).
82. See NLJ (May 11, 1987) at p. 8.
83. 119 AD2d 252 (September 29, 1986).
84. 170 Cal App 3d at pp. 556-57 (1980).
85. Infra note 67 at 182 et seg.
86. 418 US 241 (1974).
87. 106 S Ct 903 (1986).
88. 447 US 74 (1980).

8

Billboards and Political Advertising: Governmental Speech Restrictions on Private Property

8.1 BILLBOARDS AND OUTDOOR ADVERTISING

In recent years, communities across the country have imposed prohibitions on the erection of or continuance of outdoor advertising billboards. The rationale is that billboards constitute hazards to pedestrians and motorists due to their distractive features; also, it is contended, billboards are unaesthetic, particularly in residential neighborhoods. Others contend, however, that regulation of billboards constitutes an abridgement of the freedom of speech.

In 1981, the U.S. Supreme Court in Metromedia, Inc. v. City of San Diego[1] addressed the constitutionality of a billboard regulation, and found the municipal regulation to be an unconstitutional abridgement of the freedom of speech guaranteed by the First Amendment.[2] The San Diego ordinance prohibited all outdoor advertising except for on-site advertising display signs and signs falling within the following categories: government signs; bench signs at public bus stops; plaques at places of historical significance; religious symbols; signs not visible from off the property; "for sale" or "for lease" signs; signs on public or commercial vehicles; signs depicting time, temperature, and news; signs within shopping malls; signs manufactured, transported, or stored within the city, if not used for advertising purposes; approved temporary, off–premises, subdivision directional signs; and temporary political campaign signs. The avowed purpose of the ordinance was to promote traffic safety, to protect public health, safety, and welfare, and to prevent destruction of the natural beauty and environment.

The California trial court granted summary judgment for the plaintiff, holding that the ordinance constituted an unreasonable exercise of police power and a violation of the First Amendment. The California appellate court affirmed on the basis of the unreasonable exercise of state police power,[3] but the California Supreme Court reversed, stating that the San Diego ordinance furthered legitimate state police power, and there was no First Amendment violation, for the ordinance was a reasonable regulation of time, place and manner.[4] The U.S. Supreme Court reversed in a 6–3 opinion, holding that the ordinance violated the First Amendment because its exemption of on-site commercial billboards accorded a greater protection to commercial than to noncommercial speech. In effect, the ordinance reached too far into the realm of protected free speech by distinguishing between permissible and impermissible signs. The Court, in five separate opinions, recognized that billboards represent a unique method of communciation, although many have non-communicative aspects; some carry commercial messages and others noncommercial messages. Although eight members of the Court were concerned with First Amendment rights, the three-paragraph dissent of Justice Rehnquist found no First Amendment issue: "In my view, the aesthetic justification alone is sufficient to sustain a total prohibition of billboards within a community."[5] However, aesthetic considerations have not moved courts to validate anti-billboard ordinances as a basis for governmental interest; courts have preferred to remove unsightly billboards in order to protect property values, promote tourism, attract new businesses, prevent urban decay, maintain historic landmarks, and improve traffic safety.[6]

Justice Byron White, in writing the 6–3 majority opinion, pointed out that while the government has legitimate interests in controlling the non-communicative aspects of billboards, the First and the Fourteenth amendments foreclose similar regulation with respect to the communicative aspects of billboards. But San Diego's general ban on signs carrying noncommercial advertising was invalid, for the ordinance prohibits an occupant from displaying his or her own ideas or the ideas of others. Furthermore, there was outright discrimination based on the ordinance's specified exceptions, which allowed some noncommercial messages in commercial and industrial zones but banned noncommercial messages in other zones. The restrictions on protected speech are not permissible because San Diego does not favor one side over another on a subject of public controversy; nor can a prohibition of all messages carried by a particular mode of communications be upheld merely because the prohibition is rationally related to a nonspeech interest, according to the Court.[7] It is up to the Courts to protect First Amendment interests against legislative intrusion rather than to defer to rational legislative judgment. The city of San Diego may not claim that official interests outweigh private interests in noncommercial communications because its official interests are not as strong as private interests in on-site commercial advertising. In summary, the ordinance "reaches too far into the realm of protected speech" and is therefore "unconstitutional on its face."

The concurring opinion of Justice Brennan emphasized that pragmatically the ordinance[8] constituted a total ban on the use of billboards in San Diego to communicate to the public messages of general applicability, whether commercial or noncommercial. San Diego may totally ban billboards only if it can prove that a sufficiently substantial governmental interest is directly furthered by that action; but the ordinance is invalid because San Diego failed to produce evidence demonstrating that billboards actually impair traffic safety; the ordinance was not narrowly or specifically drawn to accomplish that traffic safety purpose; and San Diego failed to show that its asserted interest in aesthetics was sufficiently substantial in its commercial and industrial areas.

In Town of Carmel v. Suburban Outdoor Advertising Co.[9] the New York Appellate Division, Second Department, on April 23, 1987, scrutinized a zoning ordinance that imposed restrictions on outdoor advertising signs, such as the display of noncommercial messages, with certain exceptions. The defendant, owner of billboards that carry noncommercial messages as well as commercial messages, was ordered to remove all of its billboards. The trial court held the town ordinance to be unconstitutional, but the appellate court found that only specific portions of the zoning ordinance "unconstitutionally restrict those outdoor signs containing noncommercial speech." The court opined: "However, the [trial] court should have undertaken a thorough review of all of the provisions of the Town of Carmel Zoning Ordinance and the Town Code of the Town of Carmel concerning the regulation of outdoor signs, and should have invalidated only those specific portions of the applicable provisions of the ordinance and code which restrict outdoor signs containing noncommercial speech, which we have determined to be unconstitutional and unenforceable." It is interesting to note that the New York Appellate Division found "the applicable provisions of the town's ordinance and code are strikingly similar to those enacted by the City of San Diego which were at issue to Metromedia, Inc. v. City of San Diego."[10] While the New York trial court relied on the U.S. Supreme Court's decision in the Metromedia case, the New York appellate court went a step further and ordered the "thorough review" of all the zoning provisions. The remand required the trial court to declare "which specific portions of the provisions . . . concerning the regulation of outdoor signs unconstitutionally restrict those outdoor signs containing noncommercial speech."

It should be observed that in Berman v. Parker,[11] the highest court had recognized aesthetics as an objective in zoning but predicated its approval of the exercise of eminent domain on the use of police power for aesthetic purposes in combination with purposes of economic and social welfare.[12]

The commercial speech aspect of billboard operation is certainly protected under the First Amendment, although the noncommercial speech (which conveys political, philosophical, social, economic, and cultural ideas) is similarly protected. Billboard advertising is admittedly affirmative in nature where the purpose is communicative; but there can be also protected "symbolic speech," as where a member of Jehovah's Witness covered up the numbers on his New Hampshire license plate on religious and moral grounds, and he was wrongfully arrested under a state statute making it a misdemeanor to do so. In Wooley v. Maynard,[13] the U.S. Supreme Court described the "symbolic speech" as "compelled expression" protected under the First Amendment: "individual freedom of mind" is protected as a right not to speak or to remain silent as much as a right to speak.

8.2 POLITICAL ADVERTISING

Political advertising may be defined as the art of bringing political concepts and ideas, as well as political personages, to the public's attention. Political speech is protected under the First Amendment by the "profound national commitment to the principle that debate on public issues should be uninhibited, robust and wide-open."[14] In Lehman v. City of Shaker Heights,[15] the U.S. Supreme Court, however, ruled in 1974 that political advertisements in city buses were unconstitutional, on the ground that a bus was not a public forum, even though the bus was a public facility. The court balanced the First Amendment right of access against the government interest advanced in support of restrictions on poltical speech. The dissenting opinions rejected the government's asserted interest in protecting captive audiences on the buses from the intrusion of political advertising, reasoning that passengers are not captive since they are not forced to view the political advertisements. On the other hand, it has been held that bus terminals are proper public forums for political advertising.[16]

The sidewalks abutting the U.S. Supreme Court building in Washington, D.C., were deemed public forums for the invocation of protection of political speech in United States v. Grace.[17] The fact that the building itself was a nonpublic forum (because of the court's administrative and judicial need for undisturbed surroundings) did not preclude the sidewalks from being public forums. Public safety concerns were not sufficiently advanced by the statutory prohibition here, according to the Court.

Unquestionably, political expression is subject to government regulation if the government can show a substantial interest in such regulation, as perhaps illustrated by the transcendent objective of eliminating corruption so that public participation in the electoral process is not dampened by cynicism or alienation. Reasonable legislative proscriptions upon political speech activity have therefore generally been upheld.[18]

The political activity of federal government workers has come under fire as the government sought to justify its regulation of political speech and activity on the basis of the government's interest in fair and effective operation of government.[19] At the hub of such restraint or restriction is the

Hatch Act,[20] which forbids government employees from taking an "active part" in political management or political campaigns. The U.S. Supreme Court has held that government employees retain the right to vote as they choose and to express their opinions on all political subjects outside the context of political campaigns.[21] To allow political speech within the context of political campaigns would mean that the government employee, by virtue of his or her position, could exert political influence, as the growth of government increasingly affects the daily life of political citizens. It would demean the government and induce disrespect for its employees.[22] Furthermore, government employees must implement the will of Congress and not be swayed by directives of the political party to which they may belong outside the context of the political campaign.[23] As the highest court expressed it in Pickering v. Board of Education,[24] "The problem . . . is to arrive at a balance between the interests of the employee as a citizen, in commenting upon matters of public concern, and the interests of the government as employer, in promoting the efficiency of the public services it performs through its employees."[25] In Elrod v. Burns,[26] the Court found that the government regulation delved into the beliefs and associations of employees without a significant countervailing interest and therefore declared the regulation invalid in the face of the First Amendment.[27] Political beliefs and their reasonable expression are not subject to the dictates of the government employer.

On the other hand, a prohibition against political signs on public property was held constitutional in Members of the City Council v. Taxpayers for Vincent.[28] The majority of the highest court acknowledged that the Los Angeles ordinance deprived political groups of some incidental expression but did not promote viewpoint discrimination; the ordinance, according to the Court, served the legitimate police power of advancing aesthetic values, and certain free speech activities may be constitutionally limited. Furthermore, there was no showing that "the posting of political posters on public property is a uniquely valuable or important mode of communication." The Court concluded: "Even though political speech is entitled to the fullest possible measure of constitutional protection, there are a host of other communications that command the same respect."[29] To allow only political advertisers to use public property would be to risk arbitrary "content" discrimination, according to the Court.

There are limitations on political promises, as delineated in Brown v. Hartlage,[30] where the Kentucky Corrupt Practices Act was applied to a political promise to serve at a reduced salary made by a political candidate prior to his election. It was contended that the act barred candidates from offering voters material benefits in consideration of their votes. Thus, there was a limit on ideas political candidates may offer voters.

Political advertising in private shopping malls and the political "right of reply" statute are also important aspects of First Amendment rights. In

Robins v. Pruneyard Shopping Center,[31] according to the U.S. Supreme Court, private shopping mall owners in California were required to permit access to political advertisers; but five years later, in 1985, the New York Court of Appeals in Shad Alliance v. Smith Haven Mall[32] allowed private mall owners in New York to exclude political advertisers. The highest court in the Pruneyard Shopping Center case held that reasonable political speech, such as petitioning activities, on privately owned shopping malls was protected by the free speech provisions in the California Constitution and the state guarantees of free speech can be much broader than federal guarantees under the First Amendment. Similar decisions interpreting state constitutions to promote political speech are found in Massachusetts,[33] New Jersey,[34] Pennsylvania,[35] and Washington.[36]

On the other hand, the New York view in Shad Alliance,[37] giving the private property owner the right to exclude political advertisers under the New York Constitution, is followed in Connecticut,[38] Florida,[39] Maryland,[40] Michigan,[41] North Carolina,[42] and Oregon.[43] The thrust of this right to exclude is derived, in part, from the state constitutional holding that only state action regarding political speech is limited or restricted; there was no state action involved in the operation of the private shopping mall. Furthermore, there must not be any discrimination in favor of other forms of political speech. The highest New York court opined that although state constitutions should be interpreted so as to be meaningful in the light of new needs and changing societal values, "this can never be 'made an excuse for imposing the individual beliefs and philosophies of the judges upon other branches of government.' "[44] The point is that courts should not be social engineers unless their feet are solidly on the ground of constitutional law and logic.

In Miami Herald Publishing Co. v. Tornillo,[45] the U.S. Supreme Court was concerned about a Florida right of reply statute that required newspapers to grant political candidates equal space on which to reply to criticisms printed in the newspaper.[46] The Court found the Florida statute objectionable because the asserted right of access infringed on the First Amendment guarantee of freedom of the press. The statute was an "intrusion into the function of editors" and in effect "operates as a command . . . forbidding appellant [the editor] to publish specified matter."[47] The Court, observing that the newspaper would have to incur added expense of publication and loss of space that could be used to print other items, opined that the effect of the statute was to dampen public debate because the newspaper in the future might not so readily publish controversial political statements. Also the Court was aware that such a statute, ostensibly aimed at opening up public debate, actually abridged freedom of speech and freedom of the press, and much more the latter.

Among other interesting recent decisions on the politics of election are Tashjian v. Republican Party of Connecticut,[48] Federal Election Commission v. Massachusetts Citizens for Life,[49] and Munro v. Socialist Workers Party.[50] In Munro the highest Court upheld the State of Washington's requirement that a minor party candidate receive at least 1 percent of the primary election vote in order to be listed on the general election ballot.[51] While the ballot-access restrictions impinge on the rights of political association and effective voting, it is a reasonable State regulation to require a political candidate to show a "significant modicum" of voter support. In the Tashijian case the defendant challenged a Connecticut law requiring voters in any primary to be registered members of that party. Here the highest Court 5–4 opined that the Connecticut law infringed on the defendant's right of political association. And in the Federal Election Commission case the Court held that corporations organized solely for ideological purposes need not obey the federal law forbidding corporations from spending money on elections except through separate political action committees or PACs. The reasoning was simple, i.e., the requirement put an unconstitutional burden on a group's right to engage in election advocacy under the First Amendment.

8.3 OTHER GOVERNMENTAL SPEECH RESTRICTIONS

Nudity on the beach was the subject of People v. Hollman[52] decided by a New York court in 1986. The defendant, after being arrested twice and charged with violation of the New York Penal Law for sunbathing in the nude on a public beach, challenged his conviction on the ground that it violated his right of freedom of expression of his political beliefs. The highest New York court, in affirming his conviction, opined:

While there may be contexts in which a public display of nudity would reasonably be understood as a means of communicating an idea, it cannot be said that nude sunbathing on a beach is a form of expression likely to be understood by the viewer as an attempt to convey a particular point of view. Although defendant apparently has a specific philosophy regarding nudism, his mere nude appearance did not create a great likelihood that his philosophy would be imparted to the public. Rather, the likely message to viewers was that defendant, like many others on the beach, had doffed his clothing to enhance his comfort, acquire an even tan, or simply display his body to others. Such conduct cannot be considered sufficiently expressive to invoke the protection of the First Amendment and Article I, Section 8, of the New York State Constitution merely because its setting was a beach where nudity is commonplace.

In short, the court found that defendant's nudity exhibition was not "expressive" because "the conduct must be intended to convey a particularized message and there must be a great likelihood that, given the surrounding circumstances, the message would be understood by those who viewed it." The court concluded:

Even were we to assume that defendant's conduct was expressive, the State's ability to regulate it or even prohibit it would not be automatically foreclosed. It is clear that the First Amendment does not guarantee the right to declare one's opinion in any place, at any time and in any manner. . . . Thus, conduct may be regulated, or even prohibited. . . . It is unquestionably a permissible regulation as applied to defendant's conduct, even if it did incidentally impinge upon his chosen form of self-expression. . . . First, prohibiting public nudity is plainly within the State's police powers. Second, the statute is not aimed at suppressing the expression of opinion concerning nudity; instead it neutrally prohibits all public displays of nudity regardless of the actor's purpose. Third, the statute furthers an important governmental objective. . . . The effect of the nude bathers' repeated appearance . . . was to foreclose its use by others. . . . There is clearly an important governmental interest in providing recreational space for the citizens of this State. . . . Finally, Penal Law Section 245.01, as applied, is as narrow as it can be in order to fulfill its governmental objective. Significantly, the statute prohibits only public nudity and does not impair defendant's right to advocate Naturism by some other means.[53]

In sharp contrast thereto is City of Burlington v. New York Times Co.,[54] in which the Vermont Supreme Court in 1987 struck down the city's sidewalk obstructions ordinance under which the city had imposed a weekly fee of $5 on each of the vending boxes selling the New York Times. Not only was the ordinance void for vagueness and overbroad, but First Amendment protections of freedom of speech were deemed to apply to news racks on public sidewalks as a matter of law. Applying similar principles to New York Court of Appeals in City of New York v. American School Publications, Inc.[55] rejected that city's attempt to bar distribution bins from public sidewalks for a free magazine.[56]

NOTES

1. 453 US 490 (1981).
2. See generally 5 Haw L Rev 79 (1983).
3. 67 Cal App3d 84 (1977).
4. 610 P2d 407 (Cal., 1977).
5. Infra note 1 at p. 570.
6. See John Donnelly & Sons v. Mallar, 453 F Supp 1272 (Maine, 1978); Desert Outdoor Advertising Co. v. County of San Bernardino, 255 Cal App2d 765 (1967); and City of New Orleans v. Levy, 64 So2d 798 (La., 1953).
7. Infra note 1 at pp. 517-21.
8.

San Diego Ordinance No. 10795 (New Series), enacted March 14, 1972. The general prohibition of the ordinance reads as follows:
B. OFF-PREMISE OUTDOOR ADVERTISING DISPLAY SIGNS PROHIBITED
Only those outdoor advertising display signs, hereinafter referred to as signs in this Division, which are either signs designating the name of the owner or occupant of the premises upon which such signs are placed, or identifying such premises; or signs advertising goods

manufactured or produced or services rendered on the premises upon which such signs are placed shall be permitted. The following signs shall be prohibited:

1. Any sign identifying a use, facility or service which is not located on the premises.

2. Any sign identifying a product which is not produced, sold or manufactured on the premises.

3. Any sign which advertises or otherwise directs attention to a product, service or activity, event, person, institution or business which may or may not be identified by a brand name and which occurs or is generally conducted, sold, manufactured, produced or offered elsewhere than on the premises where such sign is located.

Section 101.0700 (F) provides as follows:

The following types of signs shall be exempt from the provisions of these regulations:

1. Any sign erected and maintained pursuant to and in discharge of any governmental function or required by any law, ordinance or governmental regulation.

2. Bench signs located at designated public transit bus stops; provided, however, that such signs shall have any necessary permits required by Sections 62.0501 and 62.0502 of this Code.

3. Signs being manufactured, transported, and/or stored within the City limits of the City of San Diego shall be exempt; provided, however, that such signs are not used, in any manner or form, for purposes of advertising at the place or places of manufacture or storage.

4. Commemorative plaques of recognized historical societies and organizations.

5. Religious symbols, legal holiday decorations and identification emblems of religious orders or historical societies.

6. Signs located within malls, court, arcades, porches, patios and similar areas where such signs are not visible from any point on the boundary of the premises.

7. Signs designating the premises for sale, rent or lease; provided, however, that any such sign shall conform to all regulations of the particular zone in which it is located.

8. Public service signs limited to the depiction of time, temperature or news; provided, however, that any such sign shall conform to all regulations of the particular zone in which it is located.

9. Signs on vehicles regulated by the City that provide public transportation including, but not limited to, buses and taxicabs.

10. Signs on licensed commercial vehicles, including trailers; provided, however, that such vehicles shall not be utilized as parked or stationary outdoor display signs.

11. Temporary off-premise subdivision directional signs if permitted by a conditional use permit granted by the Zoning Administrator.

12. Temporary political campaign signs, including their supporting structures, which are erected or maintained for no longer than 90 days and which are removed within 10 days after election to which they pertain.

9. 492 NYS2d 664, 110 AD 2d 1065 (1987).

10. Infra note 1.

11. 348 US 26 (1954).

12. Justice Douglas did, however, equate aesthetics with the concept of public welfare: "The concept of the public welfare is broad and inclusive. The values it represents are spiritual as well as physical, aesthetic as well as monetary. It is within the power of the legislature to determine that the community should be beautiful as well as healthy, spacious as well as clean, well-balanced as well as carefully patrolled."

13. 430 US 705 (1977).

14. See New York Times Co. v. Sullivan, 376 US 254 (1964) at p. 270.

15. 418 US 298 (1974).

16. See Wolin v. Port of New York Authority, 392 F2d 83 (2d Cir., 1968), cert den 393 US 940 (1968).

17. 461 US 171 (1983).

18. See Broadrick v. Oklahoma, 413 US 601 (1973), and Pickering v. Board of Education, 391 US 563 (1968).

19. For example, see United States Civil Service Commission v. National Association of Letter Carriers, 413 US 601 (1973).

20. 5 USC 7324.

21. Infra note 19; also see United Public Workers v. Mitchell, 330 US 75 (1947).

22. Infra note 19 at p. 565.

23. Id.

24. Infra note 18.

25. Id. at p. 568.

26. 427 US 347 (1976).

27. Note Clements v. Fashing, 102 S Ct 2836 (1982) on Texas's regulation of its state employees.

28. 466 US 789 (1984).

29. Id. at p. 816.

30. 456 US 45 (1982).

31. 447 US 17 (1980).

32. 488 NE2d 1211 (N.Y., 1985).

33. See Batchelder v. Allied Stores International, 445 NE2d 590 (Mass., 1983), on access to mails for voter-initiated referenda.

34. See State of New Jersey v. Schmid, 423 A2d 615 (N.J., 1980), on political advertising on university campus.

35. See Commonwealth v. Tate, 432 A2d 1382 (Pa., 1981), on political advertising on college campus.

36. See Alderwood Associates v. Washington Environmental Council, 635 P2d 108 (Wash., 1981).

37. Infra note 32.

38. See Cologne v. Westfarms Associates, 469 A2d 1201 (Conn., 1985).

39. See New York Times (February 10, 1986) at p. A12, col 1.

40. See infra note 39.

41. See Woodland v. Michigan Citizens Lobby, 378 NW2d 337 (Mich., 1985).

42. See State v. Felmet, 273 Se 2d 708 (N.C., 1981).

43. See Lenrich Associates v. Heyda, 504 P2d 112 (Ore., 1972).

44. Infra note 32 at pp. 1216-17.

45. 418 US 241 (1974).

46. See generally 64 Marq L Rev 507 (1981) at pp. 539 et seq.

47. Infra note 45 at pp. 256-58.

48. 107 S Ct 544 (1986).

49. 107 S Ct 616 (1986).

50. 107 S Ct 533 (1986).

51. A.B.A.J. (December 1, 1987) at 48-49.

52. —AD2d—,—NYS2d—(October 21, 1986).

53. Penal Law 245.01 states: "A person is guilty of exposure if he appears in a public place in such a manner that his private or intimate parts of his body are

unclothed or exposed. For purposes of this section, the private or intimate parts of a female person shall include that portion of the breast which is below the top of the areola. This section shall not apply to the breastfeeding of infants or to any person entertaining or performing in a play, exhibition, show or entertainment."

54. —A2d—(Vt., July 24, 1987).

55. 69 NY2d 576 (June 2, 1987).

56. Note City of Lakewood v. Plain Dealer Publishing Co., 794 F2d 1139 (6th Cir., 1986).

9

Picketing, Pamphleteering, Petitioning, Electioneering and the Right to Demonstrate

Freedom of speech and of expression may take diverse forms as it is exercised. Picketing, pamphleteering, petitioning, and electioneering are but a few of the forms that frequently take place on private property, such as shopping centers and shopping malls, university campuses, and corporate office complexes. Whether these forms of speech or expression are labeled political speech or commercial expression is meaningless, for the First Amendment does not distinguish between political and nonpolitical expression.[1] The right to demonstrate may encompass these diverse forms of freedom of speech or expression, as delineated in section 9.5.

In Terminello v. Chicago[2] the U.S. Supreme Court in 1949 had occasion to opine: "[Free speech] may indeed best serve its high purpose when it induces a condition of unrest, creates dissatisfaction with conditions as they are, or even stirs people to anger. Speech is often provocative and challenging. It may strike at prejudices and preconceptions and have profound unsettling effects as it presses for acceptance of an idea."

9.1 PICKETING

Picketing has generally been classified as commercial speech, though the categorization hardly befits the myriad of reasons and conveniences for picketing. Under the four-part test enunciated in Central Hudson Gas & Electric Corp. v. Public Service Commission,[3] according "a lesser protection to commercial speech than to other constitutionally guaranteed expression,"[4] it would appear that picketing permits a content-based restriction upon such commercial speech only when it "directly advances" a "substantial governmental interest" and "is not more extensive than necessary to serve that interest."[5] But Justice Douglas was more realistic in his concurring opinion in Amalagamated Food Employees Union v. Logan

Valley Plaza.[6] He observed: "Picketing is free speech plus, the plus being physical activity that implicate traffic and related matters. Hence, the latter aspects of picketing must be regulated." Interference by those picketing with employees and customers, for example, could readily be banned, but trespass laws cannot be utilized to exclude members of the public from exercising their First Amendment picketing rights, particularly on premises that are freely accessible to the public. In short, peaceful picketing by union members of a non-union business is not enjoinable as a trespass because First Amendment rights of those who picket must be protected.[7]

In Police Department of Chicago v. Mosley,[8] the U.S. Supreme Court found the Chicago ordinance that prohibited picketing on a public way within 150 feet of a grade school or a high school from one-half hour before the school was in session until one-half hour after the school session had been concluded to be in violation of the First Amendment. Although the ordinance purported to regulate the time, place, and manner[9] of speech activities in the public forum, the ordinance did so with regard to the content of the speech. Content regulation was the fatal flaw in the ordinance: "It describes permissible picketing in terms of its subjectmatter. Peaceful picketing on the subject of a school's labor-management dispute is permitted, but all other peaceful picketing is prohibited. The operative distinction is the message on a picket sign. But, above all else, the First Amendment means that government has no power to restrict expression because of its message, its ideas, its subjectmatter, or its content.

In 1980, in Cary v. Brown,[10] an Illinois statute that prohibited all picketing of residences or dwelling places except for the peaceful picketing of a place of employment involved in a labor dispute was similarly invalidated. The Court opined that the statute accorded preferential treatment to the expression of views on one particular subject and thus allowed only certain types of residential picketing based on the content of the message. But the First Amendment would not bar an antiresidential picketing statute that was uniform and nondiscriminatory in its regulation. Picketing on jailhouse grounds was banned in Adderly v. Florida[11] because jailhouses are "built for security purposes" and are not open to the public.

In 1986 in Finzer v. Barry[12] the plaintiffs, picketing the Soviet and Nicaraguan governments within 500 feet of each nation's respective embassy, sought to obtain a permanent injunction against the enforcement of a District of Columbia ordinance banning such picketing upon the ground that the ordinance violated their First Amendment rights of freedom of speech and of expression. Judge Robert Bork, writing the majority opinion based upon a 2–1 vote, upheld the ordinance upon a multitude of grounds including the obligation under international law for the United States, as host State, to protect foreign embassies. Citing the power of Congress "to define and punish . . . Offenses against the Law of Nations," the federal appellate court demonstrated that the international obligation of the federal government[13] precluded the exercise of First Amendment rights of picketing. Judge Bork declared that "the nature and extent of First Amendment rights may vary with the location at which their exercise is sought . . . the First Amendment does not guarantee an optimal setting for speech."[14] Accordingly, the District of Columbia ordinance was a permissible accomodation of the competing First Amendment and international law values. The strong dissent of Chief Judge Partricia Wald favored First Amendment rights of picketing, and she objected to the majority's use of the internationnal law obligation to justify a statute that otherwise would violate the First Amendment.[15] The dissent pointed out that the ordinance had the intent of suppressing speech in order to protect listeners who may find it distasteful, offensive or disagreeable! Indeed, according to dissent, "The U.S. Supreme Court has indicated that the Constitution tolerates, and may even require, some broader restrictions on speech in order to avoid the evil of narrower content-based classifications," i.e., the quantity of speech is not the only measure of restrictiveness.[16]

Picketing by organized unions is protected free speech unless there is rioting or mass, obstructive picketing, as explained in 1957 by Justice Douglas in his dissent in International Brotherhood of Teamsters v. Vogt.[17] Even the majority opinion of Justice Frankfurter stated that "peaceful picketing in general (is broadly assimilated) to freedom of speech, and as such protected against abridgement by the Fourteenth Amendment.[18]

9.2 PAMPHLETEERING

Pamphleteering is another activity protected by the First Amendment, as illustrated in State of New Hampshire v. Chong.[19] Here, the city ordinance prohibited the distribution of handbills, notices, or advertising devices of any other kind without a permit from the chief of police. The New Hampshire Supreme Court held that the ordinance, on its face, violated the state and federal constitutions; "prior restraints" are inherently suspect for they threaten the fundamental right to free speech. Keeping the public streets free from litter is insufficient justification, according to the court.[20] On the other hand, in Lloyd Corp., Ltd. v. Tanner[21] the distribution of handbills in Oregon protesting the draft and the Vietnam War was restrained on the ground that the shopping center was private property that had not lost its private character simply because the public used the center in 1970 for purposes of shopping. Furthermore, the handbilling was unrelated to any activity within the shopping center. There were also alternative means of communication—pamphleteering in other parts of the city and state, for example.

9.3 PETITIONING

Petitioning may involve the right to petition for a redress of grievances, a right protected under the express language of the First Amendment, or merely the solicitation and collection of signatures for any lawful purpose. In the Pruneyard Shopping Center case,[22] students were soliciting signatures to protest a United Nations resolution maliciously equating zionism with racism. The U.S. Supreme Court upheld their fundamental freedom of speech even on the private property of the shopping center. Yet in Connecticut, signature solicitation for the ratification of the equal rights amendment by the Connecticut National Organization for Women on the largest shopping mall in the state was held to be unprotected by the Connecticut Constitution in Cologne v. Westfarms Associates.[23] The Connecticut Supreme Court noted that the private shopping mall had a written policy prohibiting any unauthorized activity on its property unrelated to its shopping use. The court rested its determination on the view that the Connecticut Constitution not only required state action, which it found nonexistent, but also prohibited only governmental, not private, intrusion. In short, the Connecticut judiciary almost abdicated its role in interpreting the state constitution by refusing to decide cases involving the delicate balancing of speech and property rights. The court did not see its role as protecting individual freedom of speech or accommodating new situations with new values and standards. The court excused its conduct by reasoning that it did not want to "relegate the legislature to a subordinate role in our governmental scheme."[24] A similar position was taken in 1982 by the Michigan appellate court in Commodities Export Co. v. Detroit,[25] which found that the distribution of commercial advertisements in a private parking lot of a privately owned store is unprotected under the First Amendment. The court ignored the state guarantees of free speech, namely, "no law shall be enacted to restrain or abridge liberty of speech."[26]

The right to petition is found in Article 21, section 1, of the Universal Declaration of Human Rights: "Everyone has the right to take part in the government of his country, directly or through freely chosen representatives."[27] Article I, section 3, of the California Constitution is much more specific in declaring that "people have the right . . . to petition the government for redress of grievances." In the Pruneyard Shopping Center case,[28] that right to petition was protected, particularly because it also involves the direct initiation of change through initiative referendum and recall under the California Constitution. Soliciting and collecting signatures is vital to that process, and proponents of any political measure must have access to places where substantial numbers of persons gather on a regular basis. Once that "door" is opened for petitioning, other petitions may be circulated, as illustrated in Eastex, Inc. v. National Labor Relations Board[29] which held that since employees rightfully on their employer's property were distributing certain literature, "they had a right to distribute organizational literature . . . (some of which may be irrelevant to organizing rights) . . . for the degree of intrusion did not vary with the content of the material."

9.4 ELECTIONEERING

Electioneering overlaps pamphleteering[30] and petitioning[31] and can also be delineated under "political speech."[32] The "plus" in electioneering, however, does involve the distribution of handbills and other political literature.

Government regulation of electioneering encompasses regulation of campaign financing, as well as disclosure and reporting requirements. The Federal Election Campaign Act of 1974,[33] with amendments, inserted the federal government into the morass of political campaigning for federal office by the following provisions: the amounts contributed to or expended by the candidate or his or her campaign committee are examined; "dirty tricks" are banned; public disclosure of contributions to and expenditures by a candidate, his or her campaign committee, or individual expenditures on behalf of a candidate must be made; and public financing of all phases of presidential elections are prescribed.

It was in Buckley v. Valeo[34] that the U.S. Supreme Court in 1976 upheld the act's limitations imposed on contributions but the Court invalidated those provisions of the act relating to expenditures as impinging upon freedom of speech or expression. Campaign expenditures are "speech" and are so intrinsically related to "speech" that any regulation of such funding must be constrained by the prohibitions of the First Amendment.[35] The Court opined that "a restriction on the amount of money a person or group can spend on political communication during a campaign necessarily reduces the quantity of expression by restricting the number of issues discussed, the depth of their exploration, and the size of the audience reached. This is because virtually every means of communicating in today's mass society requires the expenditure of money."[36]

In California Medical Association v. Federal Election Commission,[37] the defendant charged the plaintiff with making contributions in excess of the amount permitted by the act. But the highest court found that the act did not violate the First Amendment even though the act imposed "far fewer restrictions on individuals and unincorporated associations than it does on corporations and unions." The point was that the act did not limit the amount that individuals may independently spend to advocate political views.

Whether the speech activity takes the form of picketing, pamphleteering, petitioning, or electioneering, there must be no discrimination among such activities. The U.S. Supreme Court in its 1980 decision in Village of Schaumburg v. Citizens for a Better Environment[38] found unconstitutional an ordinance that barred door-to-door and street solicitation by charitable organizations using less than 75 percent of their receipts for charitable purposes. Not only was the regulation too broad, but the inherent discrimination against one form of speech activity was unjustified.

9.5 THE RIGHT TO DEMONSTRATE

The right to demonstrate may be said to encompass all the rights described in picketing, pamphleteering, petitioning, and electioneering.[39] But the right to demonstrate may go much further, as exemplified by the constitutional protection afforded even extremist group demonstrations and/or parades. As a form of expression, such activity is generally protected by the First Amendment, although there are reasonable restraints that local communities, for example, may place on such conduct by extremist groups. But government has no power to restrict expression because of its message, its ideas, its subject matter, or its content.[40] To single out extremist expression for prohibition because of its offensive quality or offensive message is generally unconstitutional.[41] But "unprotected speech" is speech that advocates imminent lawless action or is likely to produce such lawless action. Government may also prohibit certain conduct performed in connection with "protected" speech, such as carrying of firearms in public demonstrations. Speech that constitutes a "clear and present danger" falls within the class of unprotected speech, which may even be punished under the appropriate criminal statute.

In Brandenburg v. Ohio,[42] the U.S. Supreme Court defined "advocacy which is directed to inciting or producing imminent lawless action and likely to incite or produce such action" as speech that poses a "clear and present danger." It is present, not future, action that is punishable; future action may be constitutionally protected since the activity does not necessarily pose a "clear and present danger."[43] The highest court in Chaplinsky v. New Hampshire[44] recognized that "fighting words," which "by their very utterance inflict injury or tend to incite an immediate breach of the peace," may also constitute speech that does not fall within the ambit of the First Amendment. In 1982, in Vietnamese Fishermen's Association v. Knights of the Ku Klux Klan,[45] the Court concluded that provocative statements made by members of a Klan paramilitary organization at a widely publicized rally constituted intimidation that was not protected speech: "The threat of violence which defendants communicated through their military activities is precisely such an irrefutable and dangerous 'communication' that it resembles the use of 'fighting words' and is therefore not protected by the First Amendment."[46]

But it should be observed that "unprotected" or unlawful speech cannot be prohibited before it is, in fact, communicated; indeed, all prior restraints are constitutionally suspect.[47] Unless it is proved that an extremist group has a specific intent to engage in unlawful activity, the assemblage or demonstration may not be enjoined.[48] But in American Civil Liberties Union v. Board of Education,[49] a California court approved the government's requirement that the applicant for a demonstration permit must state whether he knowingly intends to use the demonstration in contravention of the law. In short, extremist group demonstrations that constitute unprotected speech are, once communicated, subject to restraint or punishment.

Another aspect of the right to demonstrate is seen in the prerequisite of licensing, i.e., the State or municipality requires prior licensing or prior written permission before the demonstration can take place. In Lovell v. Griffin[50] the U.S. Supreme Court declared void "on its face" an ordinance prohibiting the distribution of "literature of any kind . . . without first obtaining written permission from the City Manager." The appellant, a Jehovah's Witness, distributed religious literature without applying for written permission. The ordinance was found by the court to be "not limited to ways which might be regarded as inconsistent with the maintenance of public order or the misuse or littering of the streets." Later in Thornhill v. Alabama[51] the court opined:

Proof of an abuse of power in the particular case has never been deemed a requisite for attack on the constitutionality of a statute purporting to license the dissemination of ideas. . . . It is not merely the sporadic abuse of power by the censor but the pervasive threat inherent in its very existence that constitute the danger to freedom of discussion. [Thus,] [o]ne who might have had a license for the asking may therefore call into question the whole scheme of licensing when he is prosecuted for failure to procure it.

In Niemotko v. Maryland[52] there existed no local law prohibiting or regulating the use of the public park in which the Jehovah's Witnesses had scheduled a demonstration; but it had been the practice for those desiring to demonstrate in the public park to obtain permission from the Park Commissioner. After being refused a license, appellants had demonstrated and were convicted of disorderly conduct. The U.S. Supreme Court found no valid basis for defendant's refusal to license the demonstration of appellants; there were "no standards . . . no narrowly drawn limitations . . . no substantial interest of the community to be served. . . . [It is] apparent that the lack of standards in the license-issuing practice rendered it a prior restraint in contravention of the Fourteenth Amendment, and that the completely arbitrary and discriminatory refusal to grant the permits was a denial of equal protection." On the other hand, as illustrated in Cox v. New Hampshire,[53] localities may devise licensing systems for demonstrations if the exercise of discretion is appropriately confined:

[T]he state court considered and defined the duty of the licensing authority and the rights of [appellants] with regard only to considerations of time, place and manner so as to conserve the public convenience. The obvious advantage [of the licensing system] was noted as giving the public authorities notice in advance so as to afford opportunity for proper policing [and serving] 'to prevent confusion by overlapping parades or processions, to secure convenient use of the streets by other travelers, and to minimize the risk of disorder.' [The state court held that the licensing board's] discretion must be exercised with 'uniformity of method of treatment [free] from [improper] consideration [and] unfair discrimination. . . . If a municipality has authority to control the use of its public streets for parades or processions, as it undoubtedly has, it cannot be denied authority to give consideration, without unfair discrimination to time, place and manner in relation to the other proper uses of the streets.

In Poulos v. New Hampshire[54] the highest court opined:

"[Appellant] objects that by the Council's refusal of a license, his right to preach may be postponed until a case, possible after years, reaches this Court for final adjudication [and argues, therefore] that he may risk speaking without a license and defeat prosecution by showing the license was arbitrarily withheld. . . . Delay is unfortunate but the expense and annoyance of litigation is a price citizens must pay for life in an orderly society where the rights of the First Amendment have a real and abiding meaning. Nor can we say that a state's requirement that redress must be sought through appropriate judicial procedure violates due process.

"[In the cases relied on by appellant, the statutes were held unconstitutional and thus] were as though they did not exist. Therefore there were no offenses in violation of a valid law. [Here] there was a valid ordinance, an unlawful refusal of a license, with remedial state procedure for the correction of the error. The state had authority to determine, in the public interest, the reasonable method for the correction of [error]. Our Constitution does not require that we approve the violation of a reasonable requirement for a license to speak in public parks because an official error occurred in refusing a proper application."

A New York City ordinance had made it unlawful to demonstrate or hold worship meetings on the street without first obtaining a permit from the police commissioner; it was also declared an offense to "ridicule or denounce any form of religious belief." In Kunz v. New York[55] the highest Court reversed a Baptist minister's conviction for engaging in scurrilous attacks upon Jews and Catholics:

"[T]here is no mention in the ordinance of reasons for which [a] permit application can be refused. This interpretation allows the police commissioner [to] exercise discretion [on] the basis of his interpretation, at that time, of what is deemed to be conduct condemned by the ordinance. We have here, then, an ordinance which gives an administrative official discretionary power to control in advance the right of citizens to speak on religious matters [on the streets]. As such, the ordinance is clearly invalid as a prior restraint on the exercise of First Amendment rights. . . .

"The court below has mistakenly derived support for its conclusion [from evidence] that appellant's religious meetings had, in the past, caused some disorder. There are appropriate public remedies to protect the peace and order of the community if appellant's speeches should result in disorder or violence. [Our concern] is with suppression—not punishment. [N]ew York cannot vest restraining control over the right to speak on religious subjects in an administrative official where there are no appropriate standards to guide his action."[56]

Under the guise of the right to demonstrate are the so-called "loud-speaker cases" involving both the right to be heard or to demonstrate as well as the right to be let alone. In Saia v. New York[57] an ordinance banned the use of sound amplification devices except for dissemination of "matters of public concern," after first obtaining permission from the local chief of police. By a 5–4 vote the U.S. Supreme Court found the ordinance to be "unconstitutional on its face" for establishing a standardless 'previous restraint' on free speech":

"The statute is not narrowly drawn to regulate the hours or places of use of loud-speakers or the volume of sound. . . . The right to be heard is placed in the uncontrolled discretion of the Chief of Police. . . . Loud-speakers are today indispensable instruments of effective public speech. The sound truck has become an accepted method of political campaigning. It is the way people are reached. [Any] abuses which [they] create can be controlled by narrowly drawn statutes. When a city allows an official to ban them in his uncontrolled direction, it sanctions a device for suppression of free communication of ideas. In this case a permit is denied because some persons were said to have found the sound annoying. In the next one a permit may be denied because some people find the ideas annoying. Annoyance at ideas can be cloaked in annoyance at sound. The power of censorship inherent in this type of ordinance reveals vice."

And in Kovacs v. Cooper[58] the highest court opined:

"City streets are recognized as a normal place for the exchange of ideas by speech or paper. But this does not mean the freedom is beyond all control. We think it is a permissible exercise of legislative discretion to bar sound trucks with broadcasts of public interest, amplified to a loud and raucous volume, from the public ways of municipalities. On the business streets of cities like Trenton, with its more than 125,000 people, such distractions would be dangerous to traffic at all hours useful for the dissemination of information, and in the residential thoroughfares the quiet and tranquility so desirable for city dwellers would likewise be at the mercy of advocates of particular religious, social or political persuasions. We cannot believe that rights of free speech compel a municipality to allow such mechanical voice amplification on any of its streets.

"[The] preferred position of freedom of speech [does] not require legislators to be insensitive to claims by citizens to comfort and convenience. To enforce free-be insensitive to claims by citizens to comfort and convenience. To enforce freedom of speech in disregard of the rights of others would be harsh and arbitrary in itself. That more people may be more easily and cheaply reached by sound trucks [is] not enough to call forth constitutional protection for what those charged with public welfare reasonably think is a nuisance when easy means of publicity are open. There is no restriction upon the communication of ideas or discussion of issues by the human voice, by newspapers, by pamphlets, by dodgers. We think that the need for reasonable protection in the homes or business houses from the distracting noises of vehicles equipped with sound amplifying devices justifies the ordinance."

The fact that loudspeakers also adversely affect a "captive audience" is still another issue that must be faced in delineating the right to demonstrate. The "rights" of the "captive audience" are perhaps best exemplified by the broadcasting media, to wit: Federal Communications Commission v. Pacifica Foundation[59] where the court stated that "although other speakers cannot be licensed except under laws that carefully define and narrow official indiscretion, a broadcaster may be deprived of his license and his forum if the FCC decided that to do so would serve the public interest, convenience and necessity."

Freedom to demonstrate has also been a topic of great concern in the state of Israel, as illustrated in Sa'ar v. Minister of Interior,[60] decided in 1980 by the Israel Supreme Court:

It is common knowledge that the jurisprudence of the State of Israel acknowledges man's basic freedoms as they are accepted in enlightened countries. The freedoms of assembly and procession are numbered among those rights. Whether we consider these freedoms to be rights in and of themselves or whether we consider them to be aspects of the freedom of expression—and there is no need for us to decide this issue—great importance is attributed to them in the fashioning of the image of a democratic regime.

Holding an assembly and a procession is one of the means at the disposal of members of the public in order to express their views on matters concerning the State, a means which at times is more effective and more tangible than other means of expression. . . .

The freedom of assembly and the freedom of procession are not unrestricted. They are relative, and not absolute, freedoms. My right to hold an assembly and procession does not mean that I have the right to go onto my friend's property without his permission, or that I am permitted to cause violence and to disturb the peace. Similar to other freedoms, here, too, it is necessary to balance the desire of the individual—and individuals—to express their views by means of assembly and procession, against the desire of the individual to protect his peace and property and the desire of the public to maintain public order and security. Without order, there is no freedom. The freedom of assembly does not mean freedom to riot.

In Israel the principal limitations on this freedom to demonstrate are set forth in a general police ordinance[61] which necessitates a license under certain conditions, and in section 151 of the Israel Penal Law, which defines an unlawful assembly as a gathering of at least three persons who conduct themselves in such a way as to give other persons reasonable grounds to fear a breach of the peace.[62] In practice, a license from the police is required when there are more than fifty people assembling outdoors to hear or discuss a speech on a political topic or to proceed together from one place to another.[63] In granting a license, the police are not granting the applicant a favor but are enabling the applicant to exercise a fundamental right. The controlling principle was set forth in the 1953 decision of the Israel High Court of Justice: "Democracy consists, first and foremost, of government by consent—the opposite of government maintained by the power of the mailed fist; and the democratic process therefore is one of selection of the common aims of the people and the means of achieving them through the public forum of negotiation and discussion, that is to say, by open debate and free exchange of ideas on matters of public interest."[64]

NOTES

1. See section 8.2 herein.
2. 337 US 1 (1949) at 4.
3. 447 US 557 (1980).
4. Quoted in Metromedia, Inc. v. City of San Diego, 453 US 490 (1981) at p. 507.
5. See generally 94 Harv L Rev 1 (1980) at p. 39.
6. 391 US 308 (1968).
7. See National Labor Relations Board v. Retail Store Employees Union, 100 S Ct 2372 (1980).
8. 408 US 92 (1972).
9. See section 2.1 herein.
10. 447 US 455 (1980).
11. 385 US 39 (1966).
12. 798 F2d 1450 (DC Cir., 1986).
13. See generally 2 Conn J of Internat L 509 (1987) at 516-517.
14. Infra note 12 at p. 1462.
15. Id. at 1482.
16. Id. at 1492.
17. 354 US 284, 77 S Ct 1166 (1957).
18. Id.
19. 435 A2d 538 (N.H., 1981).
20. According to the court, "The ordinance is particularly offensive because it gives one governmental official unfettered discretion to determine who may distribute handbills. . . . No standards guide the chief of police in deciding whether to issue a permit. The U.S. Supreme Court had consistently held statutes placing

unlimited discretion in one governmental official unconstitutional. . . . We now unhesitatingly hold that the ordinance is unconstitutional to the extent it requires standardless prior approval for distributing political leaflets (or pamphleteering)."

21. 92 S Ct 2219 (1972).
22. 447 US 17 (1980).
23. 469 A2d 1201 (Conn., 1984).
24. Infra note 23 at p. 1215.
25. 321 NW2d 842 (Mich App., 1982).
26. Mich Const (1963), Article I, section 5.
27. See 10 Golden Gate U L. Rev 805 (1980) at p. 838.
28. Infra note 22.
29. 437 US 556 (1978).
30. See section 9.2.
31. See section 9.3.
32. See section 8.2 herein.
33. Pub L 92-225, 86 Stat 3 (1971).
34. 424 US 1 (1976).
35. Note Stromberg v. California, 283 US 359 (1931).
36. Infra note 26.
37. 453 US 182 (1981).
38. 444 US 620 (1980).
39. Note sections 9.1 through 9.4.
40. See Police Department of the City of Chicago v. Mosley, 408 US 92 (1972).
41. See Collin v. Smith, 578 F2d 1197 (7th Cir., 1978), cert den 439 US 916 (1978).
42. 395 US 444 (1969).
43. See Hess v. Indiana, 414 US 105 (1973).
44. 315 US 568 (1942).
45. 543 F Supp 198 (Tex., 1982).
46. Id. at p. 208.
47. See Near v. Minnesota, 283 US 697 (1931), and Southeastern Promotions Ltd. v. Conrad, 420 US 546 (9175).
48. See generally 68 Mich L Rev 1481 (1970).
49. 59 Cal 2d 203 (1963).
50. 303 US 444, 58 S Ct 666 (1938).
51. Infra note 44.
52. 340 US 268, 71 S Ct 325 (1951).
53. 312 US 569, 61 S Ct 762 (1941).
54. 345 US 395, 73 S Ct 760 (1953).
55. 340 US 290, 71 S Ct 312 (1951).
56. The concurrence of Justice Frankfurter stated:

Kunz was not arrested for what he said [nor] because at the time he was disturbing the peace or [obstructing] traffic. He was arrested because he spoke without a license, and the license was refused because the police commissioner thought it likely on the basis of past performance that Kunz would outrage the religious sensibilities of others. If such had been the supportable finding on the basis of fair standards in safe-guarding peace, [we] would not be justified in upsetting it. It would not be censorship in advance. But here the standards are [not defined] to preclude discriminatory or arbitrary action by officials. [But] the situation here disclosed is not, to reiterate, beyond control on the basis of regulation appropriately directed to the evil.

57. 334 US 558, 68 S Ct 1148 (1948).

58. 336 US 77, 69 S Ct 448 (1949).

59. 438 US 726 (1978).

60. (1980) 34 (ii) P.D. 169 at pp. 171, 172.

61. See Police Ordinance (New Version) 5731-1971, 2 L.S.I. (N.V.) 158.

62. See 18 Israeli L Rev (1983) at pp. 511 et seq.

63. Id. at p. 513.

64. See Kol Ha'am Company Ltd. v. Minister of Interior (1953), 7 P.D. 871, 876; 1 S.J. 90 at 95 per Agranat J.

10

Pornography, Obscenity, Ethnic Slurs, and the First Amendment

Alan Dershowitz of the Harvard Law School faculty as recently as 1986 took the view that there is no precise definition of pornography, and therefore "to deny constitutional protection to a genre of speech that is incapable of precise definition is to endanger all freedom of expression."[1] Nor is the word *obscenity* definable with any precision, as illustrated in Spokane Arcades, Inc. v. Brockett,[2] where the federal appellate court overturned a Washington obscenity statute that defined obscenity in terms of "prurient interest . . . which incites lasciviousness or lust." (However, the U.S. Supreme Court in 1985 upheld that portion of the state statute prohibiting the sale or distribution of material that incites "lasciviousness" because that term is apparently definable.)[3] By the same token, the definition of ethnic slurs or racial or offensive jokes leaves much to be desired.[4] Whether Professor Dershowitz is correct in his conclusion that the lack of definition of terms "endangers all freedom of expression" remains to be seen.

10.1 PORNOGRAPHY

Pornography in the United States is a multimillion dollar business that sells "a product that is widely desired and socially significant. The industry is larger than the legitimate film and record industries combined."[5] Pornography can probably be defined as a systematic practice of exploitation and subordination based on sex that differentially harms and debases men and women.[6] In a provocative article, Margaret Baldwin addressed this issue:

The sexual requirements of men and women are perfectly congruent, symbiotic in relation, and polar in definition: women live to be fucked, men inevitably fuck.

Women especially love to be fucked by animals, dildoes, fists, and penises, especially while being bound, beaten, cut, mutilated, and killed. Women love this always, no less when we are children, than when we are adolescent, than when we are adult; no less when we are pregnant than we ourselves are born. On the rare occasions that we don't like it, we deserve it. Men inevitably fuck. Fortunately for us, they love to fuck us in all the ways we love to be fucked. This is the version of sexual equality that is in the mouths of the pornographers who tell us they love women.[7]

To combat pornography, states and localities have promulgated ordinances. The Minneapolis pornography ordinance,[8] for example, in essence seeks to redress injuries demonstrably suffered by women as a class. Pornography is said to create and maintain the civil inequality of the sexes. The ordinace endeavors to provide a private cause of action against traffickers in pornography on behalf of all women. Admittedly there are two personalities present: the moralists, who view pornography as harmful because it degrades and enfeebles the moral sensibilities of consumers, and the sexual liberationists, who view pornography as enriching sexual imagination.[9] But whether pornography merits the protection of the First Amendment is purely a legal question to be answered by the legislative, judicial, and executive branches of government.

In American Booksellers Association v. Hudnut,[10] an Indianapolis, Indiana, ordinance,[11] which purported to be a civil law against pornography, was held to be unconstitutional on three grounds: it regulated speech protected by the First Amendment; it was vague and ambiguous; and it permitted an unlawful prior restraint by an administrative committee. The federal district court still distinguished the pornography here from the lack of First Amendment protection generally assigned to obscenity,[12] to libel,[13] to words directed at inciting imminent lawlessness,[14] or to material depicting children engaged in sexual conduct.[15] While the pornography delineated in the ordinance appeared to the court to resemble obscenity, the court believed that the ordinance "spans so much more broadly with its regulatory scope than merely 'hard core' obscenity that it intrudes unlawfully on protected speech."[16] The court opined that the free speech interest of the plaintiffs outweighed the state's interest in sex-based equality.[17] The court also found that "subordination of women" in the ordinance was too vague, as were "degradation," "abasement," and "inferior." Prior restraint here violated the due process of law requisites, as described in Freedman v. Maryland.[18] Furthermore, the ordinance nowhere required a prompt judicial determination. The Seventh U.S. Court of Appeals in 1985 affirmed and held the ordinance unconstitutional on its face,[19] and the U.S. Supreme Court summarily affirmed without opinion.[20].

Antipornography ordinances differ from obscenity law in several ways. The former focuses on sexual coercion and not on sexuality per se; the former is concerned with the victim of the sexual coercion, while the latter is obsessed with the effect of the material on the consumer; and the former are civil rights measures providing civil relief, such as damages and injunctions for the victim of the sexual coercion, while the latter is for the most part criminal in scope and the government is the enforcer of the obscenity statute or law.[21]

The Oregon Supreme Court in 1987 in State v. Henry[22] construing the Oregon Constitution, decided that pornography fully merited protection: "In this State any person can write, print, say, show or sell anything to a consenting adult, even though that expression may be generally or universally 'obscene.' " The court overturned an Oregon statute that defined obscenity as offensive to contemporary standards within the state. The Oregon defendant, who was the owner of an adult bookstore, had been convicted of possessing obscene material with the purpose of disseminating the material by sale. The New York Court of Appeals in December 1986 in Arcara v. Cloud Books[23] also relied on the state constitution in holding that an adult bookstore could not be closed, even if sex acts were committed on its premises, and despite a U.S. Supreme Court pronouncement that the county could seek a court order to close the same bookstore on other grounds.[24] New York Chief Judge Sol Wachtler had echoed that "New York has a long history and tradition of fostering and supporting works which in other States could be offensive to the community . . . and the minimal national standard established by the Supreme Court for First Amendment rights cannot be considered dispositive in determining the State's constitutional guarantee of freedoms of expression."

The thrust of antipornographic attack is the professed injury to women as a class; the pornography world encompasses all women as appropriate victims.[25] But the same conclusion can be drawn for men who are victims of sexual terrorism. There is a struggle for social equality that is interrupted and even dismembered by pornography, according to the antipornographists.[26] Nevertheless, pornography for adults seems to be protected by the First Amendment, but pornography involving children is not the same, at least judging by the 1982 decision of the U.S. Supreme Court in New York Times Co. v. Ferber.[27] Here the Court held that the traditional First Amendment barriers do not prevent a state from prohibiting visual depictions of sexually explicit material involving children as performers. Such material involving children need not appeal to the prurient interest nor be patently offensive; it may be banned even if the material has literary or scientific value. The lack of First Amendment protection resulted from a balancing of the social content of the speech activity—children engaging in explicitly sexual conduct—against the potential harm to First Amendment interests: "The evil to be restricted so overwhelmingly outweighs the expressive interests, if any, at stake, that no process of case-by-case adjudication is required. When a definable class of material . . .

bears so heavily and persuasively on the welfare of children engaged in its production, . . . the balancing of interests is clearly struck and . . . it is permissible to consider these materials as without the protection of the First Amendment."[28]

In contrast, the highest court in 1985 in Brockett v. Spokane Arcades, Inc.[29] upheld the constitutionality of a "moral nuisance" statute that prohibited the public exhibition, as a regular course of business, of decidedly lewd and lascivious motion pictures. Public nuisance statutes have often served as the background for attacking pornography, provided that there has been a judicial finding of obscenity. It was in 1965 in Freedman v. Maryland[30] that the U.S. Supreme Court set forth a test for courts to utilize when deciding such public nuisance cases: (1) the burden of proving that the material is unprotected speech or expression rests on the censor; (2) only a procedure requiring a judicial determination suffices to impose a valid final restraint; and (3) the procedure must also ensure a prompt final judicial decision, to minimize the deterrent effect of an interim and possibly erroneous denial of a license.[31] It was in 1931 in Near v. Minnesota[32] that the highest court first invoked the prior restraint doctrine when it held that a statute authorizing an injunction against the publication of "obscene, lewd, and lascivious . . . or malicious, scandalous and defamatory" newspapers or other periodicals was unconstitutional. A corollary of public nuisance statutes are zoning ordinances used to curb pornography. It was in 1926 in Euclid v. Ambler Realty Co.[33] that the U.S. Supreme Court upheld a zoning ordinance that was "clearly [not] arbitrary [or] unreasonable, having . . . substantial relation to the public health, safety, morals or general welfare."[34] In the 1986 decision of City of Renton v. Playtime Theaters, Inc.,[35] the Court found that a local zoning ordinance prohibiting adult motion picture theaters from locating within 1,000 feet of any residential zone, church, park, or school to be a "valid governmental response to the serious problem created by adult theaters and satisfies the dictates of the First Amendment."

This high court decision was a reversal of the federal district court's vacation of a preliminary injunction and summary judgment for the city of Renton, Washington. The Ninth U.S. Court of Appeals reversed the district court judgment and held that the Renton ordinance was in fact a substantial restriction on freedom of speech.[36] The federal appellate court opined that the city of Renton could not properly rely on the experiences of other cities in lieu of specific evidence with regard to the effects of adult theaters on Renton. Furthermore, the city had failed to demonstrate adequately the existence of a substantial or compelling governmental interest.[37] The reversal by the U.S. Supreme Court, which made the city of Renton ordinance constitutionally sound, pointed out that since the ordinance did not impose a total ban on adult theaters, the time, place, and manner restrictions[38] are constitutionally permissible since they were "designed to serve a substantial governmental interest and do not unreasonably limit alternative avenues of communication."[39] Furthermore, the thrust of the ordinance was not with the content of the adult films but with the secondary effects of adult movie theaters on the surrounding community. Thus, the city of Renton's pursuit of its zoning interests was wholly unrelated to the suppression of free expression. Indeed, that the city of Renton

chose first to address the potential problems created by one particular kind of adult business in no way suggests that the city has "singled out" adult theaters for discriminatory treatment. We simply have no basis on this record for assuming that Renton will not, in the future, amend its ordinance to include other kinds of adult businesses that have been shown to produce the same kinds of secondary effects as adult theaters.[40]

The dissenting opinion of Justice Brennan stressed that the ordinance was content based and therefore not properly analyzed as a content–neutral time, place, and manner restriction. The dissent rejected the secondary effects of adult movie theaters, pointing out that "bars, massage parlors, and adult bookstores are not subject to the same restrictions. This selective treatment strongly suggests that Renton was interested not in controlling secondary effects associated with adult businesses but in discriminating against adult movie theaters based on the content of the films they exhibit."[41] According to the dissent, the ordinance was unconstitutional under the standards set by the highest court in Heffron v. International Society for Krishna Consciousness, Inc.[42] because it was not precisely drawn to "serve a significant governmental interest" or designed to "leave open amply alternative channels for communication of the restricted information."[43] The city of Renton failed to demonstrate through independent research that the challenged ordinance actually furthered some substantial governmental interest.[44] It should be noted that the city subsequently amended the ordinance to reduce the minimum distance allowable between an adult movie theater and any school.[45]

Pornographic photographers of children engaging in sexual activities have been convicted of pandering under the California Penal Code. In People v. Fixler,[46] the California Court of Appeals affirmed the conviction: "While First Amendment considerations may protect the dissemination of printed or photographic material regardless of the manner in which the material was originally obtained, where a crime is committed in obtaining the material, the protection afforded its dissemination would not be a shield against prosecution for the crime committed in obtaining it."

In Dallas Cowboys Cheerleaders v. Pussycat Cinema,[47] the Second U.S. Court of Appeals viewed a pornographic movie in which the distinctive uniform and emblems of the Dallas Cowboys professional football team were worn by an actress. The court readily found an appropriation of a valuable trademark. There were "numerous ways in which defendants may comment on 'sexuality in athletics' without infringing plaintiffs' trademarks." The court called the pornographic film "sexually depraved" and waved aside defendants' argument that the film was "satiric" by stating that the fact that "defendants' movie may convey a barely discernable message does not entitle them to appropriate plaintiffs' trademark in the process of conveying that message."[48] Unfortunately, the court's reliance on "taste" is contrary to First Amendment principles requiring content neutrality in evaluating literary material.[49] However, the court rested its decision on its delineation of plaintiffs' trademarks as "property rights," which did not have to "yield to the exercise of First Amendment rights under circumstances where adequate alternative avenues of communication exist."[50]

The Fourth U.S. Court of Appeals in United States v. Guglielmi, decided May 21, 1987, rejected the argument that "stag films" (in this case, graphically describing sex acts of women with a boar, a small pony, large dogs, and eels) could not be pornographic or obscene because the films were so disgusting that they could not appeal to the prurient interests of the average zoo-philiac, much less that of the average person. A federal jury had convicted the film wholesaler and distributor on eleven obscenity counts for the eight films. The federal appellate court found the films to have "the capacity to attract individuals eager for a forbidden look. . . . Those individuals need not all be average persons. . . . We simply cannot accept the proposition that the First Amendment lends no protection to offensive materials, but envelops the most offensive within its protective wings."

10.2 PROSTITUTION AND THE FIRST AMENDMENT

Prostitution and promotion of prostitution are not constitutionally protected activities.[51] State statutes making such activities criminal have generally been upheld as constitutional exercise of legislative authority.[52] In People v. Kovner,[53] the defendant was charged with promoting prostitution in the second degree, arising out of his production and sale of several explicitly sexual films. The New York court ruled that his hiring of actors and actresses for the purpose of engaging in filmed sexual conduct constituted prostitution under New York law. The state has greater power to regulate nonverbal physical contact that to suppress depictions or description of the nonverbal physical contact. New York may regulate social evils that border First Amendment rights but has the burden of establishing that its interests are legitimate and compelling, so that any incidental infringement upon First Amendment rights, if any, is no greater than essential to vindicate the state's subordinating interest. (It should be noted that in at least eight states, the patronizing of a prostitute is not legal but is not a crime.)[54]

Prostitution laws for the most part have been successfully used to prosecute pornographers because these criminal laws do meet due process requisites without unduly infringing upon First Amendment rights of speech or expression.[55]

10.3 OBSCENITY AND THE FIRST AMENDMENT

The classic obscenity case goes back to 1868 in England when Queens Bench in Regina v. Hicklin[56] characterized obscenity having a "tendency to deprave or corrupt those whose minds are open to such immoral influences." It was not until 1957 in Roth v. United States[57] that the U.S. Supreme Court made its first attempt to define obscenity. Justice Brennan, writing for the majority, stated that material is obscene (and therefore devoid of First Amendment protection) if taken as a whole, it appeals primarily to "prurient interest," defined as the "quality of being prurient; lascivious desire or thought."[58] The dissent by Justice Harlan echoed that definition as "the essential character . . . [being] to degrade sex, . . . [to] have an eroding effect on moral standards."[59] The standards by which this judgment was to be made, according to the Court, were those of the "average person" and of the "contemporary community." The test was whether "to the average person, applying contemporary community standards, the dominant theme of . . . the material taken as a whole appeals to prurient interests."[60] It took Justice Brennan sixteen years to realize that the definition, or "concept of 'obscenity,' cannot be defined with sufficient specificity and clarity to provide fair notice to persons who create and distribute sexually oriented materials, to prevent substantial erosion of protected speech as a by-product of the attempt to suppress unprotected speech, and to avoid very costly institutional harm." This important decision was Paris Adult Theatre v. Slaton,[61] which involved civil complaints seeking to have two films exhibited in petitioners' theaters declared obscene and their exhibition enjoined. The films allegedly depicted simulated fellatio, cunnilingus, and group sex intercourse. The U.S. Supreme Court vacated and remanded the case:

This is not to be read as disapproval of the Georgia civil procedure employed in this case, assuming the use of a constitutionally acceptable standard for determining what is unprotected by the First Amendment. On the contrary, such a procedure provides an exhibitor or purveyor of materials the best possible notice, prior to any criminal indictments, as to whether the materials are unprotected by the First Amendment and subject to state regulation. . . . Here, Georgia imposed no restraint on the exhibition of the films involved in this case until after a full adversary proceeding and a final judicial determination by the Georgia Supreme Court that the materials were constitutionally unprotected. . . .

We categorically disapprove the theory, apparently adopted by the trial judge, that obscene, pornographic films acquire constitutional immunity from state regulation simply because they are exhibited for consenting adults only. . . . Although we have often pointedly recognized the high importance of the state interest in regulating the exposure of obscene materials to juveniles and unconsenting adults, this Court has never declared these to be the only legitimate state interests permitting regulation of obscene material. . . .

In particular, we hold that there are legitimate state interests at stake in stemming the tide of commercialized obscenity, even assuming it is feasible to enforce effective safeguards against exposure to juveniles and to the passerby. . . .

These include the interest of the public in the quality of life and the total community environment, the tone of commerce in the great city centers, and, possibly, the public safety itself. The Hill-Link Minority Report of the Commission on Obscenity and Pornography indicates that there is at least an arguable correlation between obscene material and, crime. . . .

[Nothing] in this Court's decisions intimates that there is any "fundamental" privacy right "implicit in the concept of ordered liberty" to watch obscene movies in places of public accommodation. [W]e have declined to equate the privacy of the home relied on the *Stanley* with a "zone" of "privacy" that follows a distributor or a consumer of obscene materials wherever he goes. See *United States v. Orito,* 413 U.S. 139, 93 S.Ct. 2674, 37 L.Ed.2d 514 (1973) [holding that Congress may forbid the interstate transportation of obscene material, even by private carriage for the private use of the transporter]; *Twelve 200-Ft. Reels; Thirty-Seven Photographs* (opinion of White, J.); *Reidel.* The idea of a "privacy" right and a place of public accommodation are, in this context, mutually exclusive. Conduct or depictions of conduct that the state police power can prohibit on a public street does not become automatically protected by the Constitution merely because the conduct is moved to a bar or a "live" theatre stage. . . .

[W]e reject the claim that Georgia is here attempting to control the minds or thoughts of those who patronize theatres. Preventing unlimited display or distribution of obscene material, which by definition lacks any serious literary, artistic, political, or scientific value as communication, *Miller,* is distinct from a control of reason and the intellect. Cf. Finnis, *"Reason and Passion": The Constitutional Dialectic of Free Speech and Obscenity,* 116 U.Pa. L.Rev. 222, 229-230, 241-243.   [W]e hold that the States have a legitimate interest in regulating commerce in obscene material and in regulating exhibition of obscene material in places of public accommodation, including so-called "adult" theatres from which minors are excluded.

The dissent of Justice Brennan emphasized this position:

[The] essence of our problem in the obscenity area is that we have been unable to provide "sensitive tools" to separate obscenity from other sexually oriented but constitutionally protected speech, so that efforts to suppress the former do not spill over into the suppression of the latter. [The] resulting level of uncertainty is utterly intolerable, not alone because it makes "[b]ookselling [a] hazardous profession," *Ginsberg* (Fortas, J., dissenting), but as well because it invites arbitrary erratic enforcement of the law.

In addition to problems that arise when any criminal statute fails to afford fair notice of what it forbids, a vague statute in the areas of speech and press creates a second level of difficulty. We have indicated that "stricter standards of permissible statutory vagueness may be applied to a statute having a potentially inhibiting effect on speech; a man may the less be required to act at his peril here, because the free dissemination of ideas may be the loser."

The problems of fair notice and chilling protected speech are very grave standing alone. But it does not detract from their importance to recognize that a vague statute in this area creates a third, although admittedly more subtle, set of problems. These problems concern the institutional stress that inevitably results where the line separating protected from unprotected speech is excessively vague. [Our] experience demonstrates that almost every case is "marginal." And since the "margin" marks the point of separation between protected and unprotected speech, we are left with a system in which almost every obscenity case presents a constitutional question of exceptional difficulty. . . .

The vagueness of the standards in the obscenity area produces a number of separate problems, and any improvement must rest on an understanding that the problems are to some extent distinct. First, a vague statute fails to provide adequate notice to persons who are engaged in the type of conduct that the statute could be thought to proscribe. The Due Process Clause of the Fourteenth Amendment requires that all criminal laws provide fair notice of "what the State commands or forbids." [E]ven the most painstaking efforts to determine in advance whether certain sexually oriented expression is obscene must inevitably prove unavailing. For the insufficiency of the notice compels persons to guess not only whether their conduct is covered by a criminal statute, but also whether their conduct falls within the constitutionally permissible reach of the statute.

The approach requiring the smallest deviation from our present course would be to draw a new line between protected and unprotected speech, still permitting the States to suppress all material on the unprotected side of the line. In my view, clarity cannot be obtained pursuant to this approach except by drawing a line that resolves all doubts in favor of state power and against the guarantees of the First Amendment. We could hold, for example, that any depiction or description of human sexual organs, irrespective of the manner or purpose of the portrayal, is outside the protection of the First Amendment and therefore open to suppression by the States. That formula would, no doubt, offer much fairer notice [and] give rise to a substantial probability of regularity. . . .

Given these inevitable side-effects of state efforts to suppress what is assumed to be *unprotected* speech, we must scrutinize with care the state interest that is asserted to justify the suppression. For in the absence of some very substantial interest in suppressing such speech, we can hardly condone the ill-effects that seem to flow inevitably from the effort. . . .

In short, while I cannot say that the interests of the State—apart from the question of juveniles and unconsenting adults—are trivial or nonexistent, I am compelled to conclude that these interests cannot justify the substantial damage to constitutional rights and to this Nation's judicial machinery that inevitably results from state efforts to bar the distribution even of unprotected material to consenting adults. I would hold, therefore, that at least in the absence of distribution to juveniles or obstrusive exposure to unconsenting adults, the First and Fourteenth Amendments prohibit the state and federal governments from attempting wholly to suppress sexually oriented materials on the basis of their allegedly "obscene" contents. Nothing in this approach precludes those governments from taking action to serve what may be strong and legitimate interests through regulation of the manner of distribution of sexually oriented material.

In 1973 in Miller v. California,[62] the highest court addressed the obscenity issue and essentially authorized the lower courts to define obscenity according to local standards. But the Court did adopt the three-tier test of standards in the Roth case,[63] that is, whether the average person applying community standards would find that the particular material appeals to the prurient interest, whether the material depicts in a "patently offensive way" sexual conduct specifically defined by applicable state law, and whether the material as a whole lacks serious literary, artistic, political, or scientific value.[64]

This three-tier test has only added to the confusion concerning definiton of terms. For example, whose "community standards" are to be applied: those of the immediate locality or those of the state at large? If the trier of fact applies the "community standards" of the state at large, can any of such findings be upset on appeal when the appellate court cannot determine from the record what was offensive to the judge at the trial level?[65] Another example of confusion surrounding definition relates to prurient interests. In 1984 in Richards v. State of Indiana,[66] the conviction of the defendant for distributing obscene material in violation of the Indiana statute was upheld by referring to notions of normality and healthiness. The Indiana appellate court accepted the trial courts instruction to the jury that "an interest in sex is normal;" but if the particular material appeals to an abnormal interest in sex, it can appeal to the prurient interest and thus be obscene within the meaning of the state statute. The court never did answer the query, What degree of such an interest in sex is in fact healthy? And the court's determination appears to be at odds with the attempted "objective test" in both the Roth[67] and Miller[68] cases. In 1974 in Jenkins v. Georgia,[69] the U.S. Supreme Court rejected the state of Georgia's attempt to classify the film *Carnal Knowledge* as obscene; nudity itself is insufficient, in the absence of exhibition of the actor's genitals or explicit depiction of ultimate sexual acts, according to the Court. Three years earlier in Eisenstadt v. Baird,[70] the Court had held that an unmarried person's fundamental right to privacy protected his or her right to have access to information about birth control, whether deemed to be obscene or not obscene.

The U.S. Supreme Court on May 4, 1987, in Pope v. Illinois,[71] somewhat resolved the confusion over the definition of obscenity by holding that judges and juries should not use contemporary community standards to determine whether sexually oriented materials have literary, artistic, political, or scientific value and therefore are not obscene. By a 6–3 vote, the majority of the Court ruled that the standard is whether a "reasonable man" would find that the allegedly obscene material has redeeming value and thus should receive First Amendment protection from state obscenity laws. Justice White agreed, however, that the first two tests delineated in Miller v. California[72] should still be examined under community standards but not the third test: whether, as a whole, the material lacks literary, artistic, political, or scientific value: "Just as the ideas a work represents need not obtain majority approval to merit protection, neither, insofar as the First Amendment is concerned, does the value of the work vary from community to community based on the degree of local acceptance it has won. . . . The proper inquiry is not whether an ordinary member of any given community would find serious literary, artistic, political or scientific value in allegedly obscene material, but whether a reasonable person would find such value in the material taken as a whole." This objective standard for the third test is, admittedly, confusing, as expressed by Justice Antonin Scalia, who wrote a separate concurring opinion: "I must note, however, that in my view it is quite impossible to come to an objective assessment of literary or artistic value, there being many accomplished people who have found literature in Dada and art in the replication of a soup can." The dissent of Justice Stevens simply stated that the standard of the "reasonable person" was much too vague.

Literature has frequently run afoul of obscenity statutes at given periods of time. Edmund Wilson's *Memoirs of Hecate County,* resplendent with passages describing sexual intercourse, inextricably related to the novel's literary merit, resulted in 1947 in the conviction of the publisher under the New York obscenity statute.[73] A year later, Pennsylvania cracked down on such classic novels as James T. Farrell's *Studs Lonigan,* William Faulkner's *Sanctuary,* and Erskine Caldwell's *God's Little Acre.*[74] Today, forty years later, these same books are not considered obscene; indeed, they occupy prominent places on any college English major's required reading list. Justice Douglas just three years earlier had observed that:

under our system of government there is an accommodation for the widest varieties of tastes and ideas. What is good literature, what has educational value, what is refined public information, what is good art, varies with individuals as it does from one generation to another. There doubtless would be a contrariety of views concerning Cervantes' 'Don Quixote,' Shakespeare's 'Venus and Adonis,' or Zola's 'Nana.' But a requirement that literature or art conform to some norm prescribed by an official smacks of an ideology foreign to our system.[75]

And eleven years later in the Roth case,[76] the U.S. Supreme Court opined that "all ideas having even the slightest redeeming social importance—unorthodox ideas, controversial ideas, even ideas hateful to the prevailing climate of opinion—have the full protection of the guarantees of the First

Amendment, unless excludable because they encroach upon the limited area of more important interests. But implicit in the history of the First Amendment is the rejection of obscenity as utterly without redeeming social importance." Yet in 1969 in Stanley v. Georgia,[77] the Court held that obscenity in the home is protected:

It is now well established that the Constitution protects the right to receive information and ideas. . . . This right to receive information and ideas, regardless of their social worth, . . . is fundamental to our free society . . . [and] also fundamental is the right to be free, except in very limited circumstances, from unwanted governmental intrusions into one's privacy. . . . Whatever may be the justification for other statutes regulating obscenity, we do not think they reach into the privacy of one's home. If the First Amendment means anything, it means that a State has no business telling a man, sitting alone in his own house, what books he may read or what films he may watch. Our whole constitutional heritage rebels at the thought of giving government the power to control men's minds.

A note writer in the Yale Law Journal in 1971 summed it up as follows:

The right to read or observe what one pleases necessarily implies the right to receive and therefore to possess all constitutionally protected materials. If an individual is deterred from acquiring and possessing a non-obscene book because he fears that it may be obscene and that he will be punished for its possession, his right to "read or observe what he pleases" has been utterly "inhibited." The First Amendment will not tolerate any law which causes a man returning home from his local bookstore to wonder whether his latest purchase may lead to his arrest.[78]

These words were more than thirty years too late for the lack of First Amendment protection afforded such literary accomplishments as *The First Lady Chatterly*[79] and *Strange Fruit*,[80] which in the 1940s were banned as obscene writings in New York and in Massachusetts. The theme of the former book was found to be wrongful gratification of sexual desires, and the theme of the latter book was the harm to the public offered by its fifty episodes of indecent sexual acts.

Despite the fact that obscenity is not protected by the First Amendment, the Second U.S. Court of Appeals recently, in Carlin Communications, Inc. v. FCC,[81] ruled that courts must scrutinize regulations affecting the determination of obscenity so as to show "a compelling governmental interest." Here, the FCC, in its effort to ban "dial-a-porn" telephone services, promulgated time, place, or manner restrictions that the court found to be aimed at "inherent dangers" of regulating speech; that is, the regulations were content based since they did not cover nonobscene or nonindecent materials.[82] The FCC here had failed to show that the regulations were well tailored to protect children from "salacious matter"; also the regulations were over inclusive because adults, in addition to minors, were denied access during certain hours to the dial-a-porn and underinclusive because minors could access the service during the hours the regulations permitted obscene messages.

10.4 ETHNIC, RACIAL, AND OTHER OFFENSIVE SLURS

The *New York Times* (April 16, 1987) reported that at the University of Michigan, ethnic, racial, and other slurs or jokes offensive to specific groups were put into a computer by students and that the university authorities and the students were trying to reconcile free speech and good taste.[83] According to the report, "Using the computer system, anyone with a password can open an electronic file for campus use and can restrict, or freeze, that file whenever that is desired."[84] Some colleges, including Dartmouth and Carnegie-Mellon, have imposed codes of ethics for students using their computers, with violators facing removal from the computer system: "Obscenities should not be sent by computer nor stored where they could offend other users."

The presence of ethnic, racial, and other offensive slurs is nothing new, as the U.S. Supreme Court delineated in its 1978 decision in FCC v. Pacifica.[85] Here the FCC recorded a monologue over radio station WBAI by comedian George Carlin, whose routine was about "the swear words, the cuss words, and the words you can't say" on the air.[86] The FCC deemed these offensive slurs to be indecent and possibly obscene, and the highest court agreed that the First Amendment did not deprive government of all power to restrict the broadcasting of indecent language regardless of circumstances. The FCC's censorship was justified on the grounds that there was an intrusion of the offensive broadcast into the home and that there were unsupervised children in the listening audience. Furthermore, the Court pointed out, the listener in the home should not be put to even the minimal discomfort of enduring offensive speech for the short interval required to change the dial or turn off the radio. The indecent language was potentially degrading and harmful to children, and governmental interest was sufficient to inconvenience those parents who wished to hear the indecent language. (Willing adults could hear Carlin's words on tapes or records or at theaters or nightclubs.) Thus, the highest court upheld in the abstract the power of the FCC to maintain standards of decency on the airwaves without any guidelines other than banning "seven dirty words."

The Federal Communications Commission (FCC) on April 29, 1987 released "new standards that the Commission will apply in enforcing the prohibition against obscene and indecent transmissions."[87] "Indecency" is defined in a generic sense as "language or material that depicts or describes, in terms patently offensive as measured by contemporary community standards for the broadcast medium, sexual or excretory activities or organs."[88] In the context of ethnic, racial, and other offensive slurs it will be interesting to see what action the FCC takes with respect to radio and TV transmissions. However, ethnic and racial and other offensive slurs or jokes, if sufficiently humorous or fun provoking, have a chance to be protected under the First Amendment. In Frank v. National Broadcasting Co.,[89] the plaintiff, a tax consultant and accountant, sued in libel the broadcaster for allegedly holding plaintiff up to ridicule and otherwise damaging his professional reputation. It seems that a skit on a particular program portrayed a character, "Fast Frank," who declared a houseplant as a dependent, took an acne treatment as an oil-depletion allowance, declared his wife's leaving him as a home improvement and took as a medical expense the paper cut he sustained while preparing his own tax return. The New York court, in dismissing the suit, was cognizant of its duty of balancing the plaintiff's right to protect his good name against the possible infringement of defendant's First Amendment rights. The court pointed out that humor has never been given absolute First Amendment protection: "Indeed, the danger implicit in affording blanket protection to humor or comedy should be obvious, for surely one's reputation can be as effectively and thoroughly destroyed with ridicule as by any false statement of fact." But the court concluded that "no person of any sense could take the so-called advice of 'Fast Frank' seriously. . . . [Furthermore, the statements were not] so malicious or vituperative that they would cause a person hearing them to hold the plaintiff in public contempt, ridicule, or disgrace." The lunacy of the statements themselves, presented as a small comic part of a larger and obviously comic entertainment program, coupled with the fact that they were neither a malicious nor a vicious personal attack, required a finding, according to the court, that they were not defamatory as a matter of law.

Another aspect of ethnic, racial and other offensive slurs is the effect of such utterances upon children. The U.S. Supreme Court addressed this point in its 1972 decision in Grayned v. City of Rockford.[90] Here the city ordinance restricted noisy demonstrations or parades or, in fact, "adult speech" on public or private property next to any building in which school is in session. The Court ruled that "such expressive conduct may be constitutionally protected at other places or other times . . . but next to a school, while classes are in session, it may be prohibited."[91] Justice Marshall, writing for the 8–1 majority in upholding the ordinance against vagueness and overbreadth challenged, pointed out that

"[G]overnment has no power to restrict [expressive] activity because of its message [but] reasonable 'time, place and manner' regulations may be necessary to further significant governmental interests, and are permitted. For example, two parades cannot march on the same street simultaneously, and government may allow only one. A demonstration or parade on a large street during rush hour might put an intolerable burden on the essential flow of traffic, and for that reason could be prohibited. If overamplified loudspeakers assault the citizenry, government may turn them down.

"The nature of a place, 'the pattern of its normal activities, dictates the kinds of regulations of time, place, and manner that are reasonable.' Although a silent vigil may not unduly interfere with a public library, *Brown,* making a speech in the reading room almost certainly would. That same speech should be perfectly appropriate in a park. The crucial question is whether the manner of expression is basically incompatible with the normal activity of a particular place at a particular time. Our cases make clear that in assessing the reasonableness of regulation, we must weigh heavily the fact that communication is involved; the regulation must be narrowly tailored to further the State's legitimate interest. 'Access to [the streets, sidewalks, parks, and other similar public places] for the purpose of exercising [First Amendment rights] cannot constitutionally be denied broadly. . . .' [*Logan Valley*] Free expression 'must not, in the guise of regulation, be abridged or denied.'

"In light of these general prinicples, we do not think that Rockford's ordinance is an unconstitutional regulation of activity around a school . . .

Just as *Tinker* made clear that school property may not be declared off-limits for expressive activity by students, we think it clear that the public sidewalk adjacent to school grounds may not be declared off-limits for expressive activity by members of the public. But in each case, expressive activity may be prohibited if it 'materially disrupts classwork or involves substantial disorder or invasion of the rights of others.' "

To the same effect was the 1986 decision of the highest court in Bethel School District No. 403 v. Fraser,[92] which rebuffed a student's challenge to a school disciplinary rule, holding that the school's infringement of his freedom of speech did not violate the First Amendment.[93] The student had made a speech in front of the student body that included repeated use of a sexual metaphor. According to the court, "constitutional rights of students in public school are not automatically coextensive with the rights of adults in other settings."[94] Thus, the possible adverse effect of such utterances upon children undoubtedly gave sanction to the power of school boards to regulate and even punish students' speech.

The same approach had been taken by the highest Court in its 1942 decision in Chaplinsky v. New Hampshire,[95] where in the course of proselytizing on the city streets the appellant, a Jehovah's Witness, denounced organized religion and cursed the city marshal, "You are a God-damned racketeer" and "a damned Fascist." The appellant was arrested and convicted under a state statute forbidding anyone to address "any offensive, derisive, or annoying word to any other person who is lawfully in any public place or calling him by any offensive or derisive name." In essence, the state statute banned "words likely to cause an average addressee to fight" or "face-to-face words plainly likely to cause a breach of the peace by the addressee." In upholding the conviction, the Court deemed it "unnecessary to demonstrate" that appellant's epithets were:

"likely to provoke the average person to retaliation. . . . There are certain well-defined and narrowly limited classes of speech, the prevention and punishment of which have never been thought to raise any Constitutional problem. These include the lewd and obscene, the profane, the libelous, and the insulting or 'fighting' words—those which by their very utterance inflict injury or tend to incite an immediate breach of the peace. [S]uch utterances are no essential part of any exposition of ideas, and are of such slight social value as a step to truth that any benefit that may be derived from them is clearly outweighed by the social interest in order and morality."

In sharp contrast thereto is the Court's earlier opinion in Cantwell v. Connecticut,[96] where another Jehovah's Witness was convicted of religious solicitation without a permit and also convicted for breach of the peace. In setting aside both convictions, the Court invalidated the permit system for religious solicitation; on the breach of peace count, the Court pointed out that the offense covered much protected speech conduct and left

"too wide a discretion in its application. . . . One may, however, be guilty of [breach of the peace] if he commits acts or makes statements likely to provoke violence and disturbance of good order. [I]n practically all [such decisions to this effect], the provocative language [held to constitute] a breach of the peace consisted of profane, indecent or abusive remarks directed to the person of the hearer. *Resort to epithets or personal abuse is not in any proper sense communication of information or opinion safeguarded by the Constitution,* and its punishment as a criminal act [under a narrowly drawn statute] would raise no question under that instrument."

10.5 CABLE TELEVISION

Cable television has also fallen prey to the confusion surrounding definitions of pornography and obscenity, particularly since many states have endeavored to legislate morality for cable television. In Utah, for example, the Utah Cable Television Programming Act[97] treats the showing by cable television systems or pay-for-viewing television programming of "indecent material" as a nuisance punishable by fines and money forfeitures. Under the act, "indecent material" includes the "visual or verbal depiction or description of human sexual or excretory organs or functions, including exposure of genitals, pubic area, buttocks, or the showing of any portion of the female breast below the top of the nipple."[98] The depiction is prohibited if the "average person applying contemporary community standards for cable television . . . would find it is presented in a patently offensive way for the time, place, manner and context.[99] In Jones v. Wilkinson,[100] the Tenth U.S. Court of Appeals ruled that although federal law preempts state regulation of the content of cable television programming, cable operators "may still be liable by a State for violating 'obscenity . . . or other similar laws.'"[101] But the federal district court here had found that the Utah statute had exceeded this limited power of dealing with obscenity, and therefore the federal law preempted the Utah statute. The concurring opinion of Judge Baldock on the circuit court agreed that the Utah statute was "both vague and overbroad," but he preferred to argue that the federal statute did not preempt state regulation: "Nor do I agree that the First Amendment forecloses the regulation of indecency on cable television, provided that the regulation is a time, place and manner restriction that is narrowly drawn and exists for the protection of minors." He favored imposing civil liability under the Utah act on cable operators for indecent programming, citing FCC v. Pacifica,[102] in which the U.S. Supreme Court observed the intrusive nature of broadcasting and its location in the homes and therefore called for greater regulation of patently offensive, indecent material. The U.S. Supreme Court in 1987 affirmed the ruling of the Tenth U.S. Court of Appeals that the Utah statute aimed at "indecent" material was unconstitutional in violating the First Amendment.[103] The thrust of the highest Court's decision is that the concept that material that is not obscene but is nonetheless considered "indecent," may receive less First Amendment protection than any other speech.[104] However, the Utah cases beginning with Home Box Office, Inc. v. Wilkinson[105] and Community Television of Utah, Inc. v. Roy City[106] have resulted in declarations of unconstitutionality.

In Cruz v. Ferre[107] the Eleventh U.S. Court of Appeals had occasion to point out that "one of the keys to the very existence of cable television is the fact that cable programming is available only to those who have cable attached to their television sets." In short, choice is what cable is all about![108] Therefore, cable is less "pervasive" than TV or radio, and different rules on indecency and obscenity might conceivably be applied: "This interest [in protecting children] is significantly weaker in the context of cable television [than in the context of broadcast television] because parental manageability of cable television greatly exceeds the ability to manage the broadcast media."

The degree of First Amendment protection that will be accorded cable television was delineated in City of Los Angeles v. Preferred Communications, Inc.,[109] where the U.S. Supreme Court affirmed that determination of the Ninth U.S. Court of Appeals holding that the city could not limit access to a single cable television company by use of an auction process when there was sufficient excess physical and economic capacity to handle another system. Unlike broadcasting, there is a lack of physical scarcity of cable television channels. Cable television operators engage in First Amendment activities, however, not only by producing original programming but also by exercising editorial discretion over all other programming. Judge Baldock's concurring opinion also cited Community Communications Co., Inc. v. City of Boulder[110] where the same court had concluded that cable broadcasting was very different from newspaper publishing where little government regulation was constitutionally permitted.

The federal appellate court in Judge Baldock's concurring opinion reiterated essential facts found by the federal district court that "are essential in deciding the degree of permissible content-based regulation:"

9. A cable television system is a non-broadcast facility consisting of a system of privately-owned coaxial cables and associated signal generation, reception and vision and other programming to subscribers.

10. Cable television service, such as that provided by [the cable operator plaintiffs], is legally available only on the premises of persons who choose to subscribe to this service and agree to establish and maintain a physical connection between their television receivers and a cable television system.

11. Television receivers that are not physically connected to a cable television system are not capable of receiving programming that is distributed solely over such a system.

12. The primary cable service offered to subscribers of [the cable operator plaintiffs] is called basic cable service. The basic cable service subscription price may include, depending on the particular system, retransmissions of the local television broadcast channels . . . plus additional television broadcast channels imported by satellite to terrestrial transmissions from distant cities (KWGN-Denver, KTVU-Oakland, KTXL-Sacramento, WTBS-Atlanta, WGN-Chicago and WOR-New York), plus special just-for-cable channels (ESPN, USA, CNN, SNC, MTV, NN, CBN, CHN, C-Span, and University of Utah ITV).

13. In addition to their basic cable service, [the cable operator plaintiffs] offer to provide programming such as that distributed by HBO (which includes recently released, feature length motion picture films, special entertainment programming and sports events) to those subscribers who choose to subscribe to this programming and to pay a monthly subscription fee in addition to the monthly fee paid for basic cable service.

14. HBO Service and pay television program services offered by companies other than HBO, including such services as Showtime, the Movie Channel and the Disney Channel, are provided by [the cable operator plaintiffs] and other cable system operators.

15. Each pay television program service offered by [the cable operator plaintiffs] and other cable system operators is offered over a separate channel, and cable subscribers may choose to receive any or all of these program services.

16. [The cable operator plaintiffs] presently have about 60,000 subscribers in Utah.

17. Cable subscribers may obtain, either at no cost or at a cost not to exceed $20.00, a "lockbox" which is key operated and attaches to the television set. These

lockboxes enable subscribers to render their sets incapable of receiving any particular channel. Such devices, while available, are not widely utilized by subscribers."

Judge Baldock opined that

indecency differs from obscenity in that indecency need not appeal to the prurient interest and, when the number of children in the audience has not been reduced to a minimum, it is not protected by a claim that it has literary, artistic, political or scientific value. . . . Not only does cable television come directly into the home, it frequently is viewed without any effective advance warning of patently offensive, indecent material. . . . It is unreasonable to shift an affirmative duty onto every parent to study all cable television program listings each week, even assuming that such listings provide adequate warning. . . . The State may restrict access to sexually oriented material which is not obscene provided that there is not an outright ban. This is to protect both the State's interest in the well-being of children . . . and the right of parents to direct the upbringing of their children.

Judge Baldock also found the Utah statute "void for vagueness":

Defining indecency with express reference to 'the time, place, manner and context in which the material is presented,' without more, would cause people of common intelligence to guess at the meaning of indecency and differ as to the law's application. . . . This uncertain meaning does not provide fair notice of what is proscribed, could result in arbitrary enforcement and could deter protected expression.

10.6 HOW ENGLAND HANDLES THE PROBLEM

In England, censorship of writings, dramas, and film on the ground of morality is generally achieved by applying the standard of obscenity or that of indecency.[111] Obscenity appears to be defined in terms of a likelihood to deprave and corrupt; indecency merely embarrasses the sexual modesty of ordinary people. Obscenity is criminally punishable under the Obscene Publications Act, 1959 as an offense of actual "publishing," such as a sale to a customer or giving the obscene matter to another person, or as an offense to possess an obscene article for publication for gain (contrary to the Obscene Publications Act, 1964). Mere possession of an obscene book, for example, is not an offense.[112] "Publishing" excludes "anything done in the course of television or sound broadcasting";[113] but a video cassette is an "article" for purposes of both acts.[114]

Since the acts are criminal in nature, the primary query is one of intent, as articulated in Regina v. Salter & Barton,[115] where two actors were charged with "aiding and abetting" the commission of the crime by performing in an obscene movie. Their conviction was upheld even though they denied any knowledge of the producer's distribution scheme. The English Court of Appeal ruled that ignorance was no excuse, for both defendants did nothing for more than two years after discovering that the obscene film was being distributed in England. Interestingly, section 4 of the acts provides the defense of "public good"; that is, the obscene publication is justified as being for the public good. As the 1976 Law Commission Report on Conspiracy and Criminal Law Reform report stated, the "publication" was "in the interests of science, literature, art or learning, or of other objects of general concern."[116] In short, a publication of obscene primitive art may lack objective merit but may be defended as a contribution to art history.[117] Frequently a jury decides this question of fact as to whether the product is indeed a product of scholarship. "Art" comprehends the application of skill to any aesthetic object or subject and is not conventionally confined to the reproduction of beautiful images.[118] But in DPP v. Jordan,[119] the House of Lords ruled that the psychiatric health of the community was not served by therapeutic pornography as an "object of general concern."

In contrast is the standard of indecency, which means that promoters of indecent material will generally not be prosecuted, provided the mails are not used, it is not imported from overseas, or it is not flaunted openly in public places.[120] In such instances, there is a possibility of prosecution under the Obscene Publications Acts, which define obscenity, in terms of likelihood to corrupt "persons who are likely, having regard to all relevant circumstances, to read, see, or hear the matter contained or embodied in it." But in Regina v. Clayton & Halsey[121] the prosecutor's argument that the material was "inherently obscene" was rejected because the defendant bookshop owner had sold the objectionable material to two policemen from Scotland Yard's Obscene Publications Squad. The officers conceded that pornography had ceased to arouse any feelings whatsoever. Indecency laws are said not to have any effect in England on freedom of expression, for their prime purpose is to maintain decorum in public places. In Knuller v. DPP,[122] the English court pointed out that "indecency is not confined to sexual indecency; indeed it is difficult to find any limit short of saying that it includes anything which an ordinary decent man or woman would find to be shocking, disgusting or revolting." But "public decency must be viewed as a whole, and the jury should be invited, where appropriate, to remember that they live in a plural society, with a tradition of tolerance towards minorities."[123] In Wiggins v. Field,[124] the concern was over a public reading of Allen Ginsberg's poem "America," which included the line, "Go fuck yourself with your atomic bomb." The court decided that in the work of a recognized poet, read without any intention of causing offense, the word *fuck* could not be characterized as "indecent": "Whether a word or phrase was capable of being treated as indecent language depended on all the circumstances of the case, the occasion, when, how, and in the course of what it was spoken and perhaps to a certain extent what the intention was."

An anomaly in English law is the crime of blasphemy, or outrageous comments about God, holy personages, or articles of the Anglican faith; blasphemy amounts to vilification, ridicule, or indecency. In Whitehouse v. Lemon,[125] the defendant published a poem about a homosexual's conversion to Christianity, which metaphorically attributed homosexual acts to Jesus Christ. Explicit references were made to acts of sodomy and fellatio. Conviction of the editor and publisher by a jury was upheld by the House of Lords because the blasphemy was expressed in an outrageously indecent or scurrilous manner. However, a defense is provided by section 7 of the Libel Act 1843 if the decision to publish the blasphemy was made without knowledge, without negligence, and without consent.[126]

According to the *New York Times* (December 19, 1987), England has today eroded press freedom by the government's legal actions against newspapers and broadcasters:

Throughout the year, the Government pursued its efforts to inhibit British publication of and news reporting about "Spycatcher," an account of misconduct in the British security services by Peter Wright, a former intelligence agent. At the same time, in less publicized cases, it has used the Police and Criminal Evidence Act to look for evidence in the news and photo libraries of newspapers, and it has turned to another restrictive statute to try to compel a financial reporter to serve as a police informant in an insider trading case.

These actions are among nine areas of legal activity directed against the press that have been identified by the Press Council, an ombudsman group financed by the newspaper industry. "With all these, Britian is sinking further into that league of nations where press freedom is barely understood, let alone protected."[127]

The article pointed out that

Whereas the First Amendment serves as a roadblock to attempts by Congress or the courts to curb the American press, Britain has no written constitution defining basic rights and restraining the Government's power to interfere. In addition, the 1689 Act of Settlement guarantees "parliamentary sovereignty." This means that the Government can lose a case in the courts and, if it has the votes in Parliament, immediately pass a new law to regain what it has lost in court.

NOTES

1. See ABAJ (November 1, 1986) at p. 36.
2. 725 F2d 482 (9th Cir., 1984).
3. 105 S Ct 2794 (1985).
4. See section 10.4.

5. See 37 Syracuse L Rev 977 (1986), quoting from 133 U Pa L Rev 497 (1985) at p. 517.

6. See 27 Ariz L Rev (1985) at p. 417 et seq.

7. See 2 Law and Inequality 629 (1984) at p. 632.

8.

Minneapolis, Minn. Code of Ordinances, Title 7, ch 139 (1982):

An Ordinance of the City of Minneapolis
(As passed by the City Council and Vetoed by the Mayor)

Amending Title 7, Chapter 139 of the Minneapolis Code of Ordinances Relating to Civil Rights: In General.

The City Council of the City of Minneapolis do ordain as follows:

Section 1. That Section 139.10 of the above-entitled ordinance be amended to read as follows:

139.10 *Finding, declaration of policy and purpose.*

(a) *Findings.* The council finds that discrimination in employment, labor union membership, housing accommodations, property rights, education, public accommodations and public services based on race, color, creed, religion, ancestry, national origin, sex, including sexual harassment and pornography, affectional preference, disability, age, marital status or status with regard to public assistance or in housing accommodations based on familial status adversely affects the health, welfare, peace and safety of the community. Such discriminatory practices degrade individuals, foster intolerance and hate, and create and intensify employment, sub-standard housing, under-education, ill health, lawlessness and poverty, thereby injuring the public welfare.

(1) *Special Findings on Pornography:* The council finds that pornography is central in creating and maitaining the civil inequality of the sexes. Pornography is a systematic practice of exploitation and subordination based on sex which differentially harms women. The bigotry and contempt it promotes, with the acts of aggression it fosters, harm women's opportunities for equality of rights in employment, education, property rights, public accommodations and public services, create public harassment and private denigration, promote injury and degradation such as rape, battery and prostitution and inhibit just enforcement of laws against these acts, contribute significantly to restricting women from full exercise of citizenship and participation in public life, including in neighborhoods, damage relations between the sexes, and undermine the women's equal exercise of rights to speech and action guaranteed to all citizens under the Constitutions and laws of the United States and the state of Minnesota.

(b) *Declaration of policy and purpose.* It is the public policy of the City of Minneapolis and the purpose of this title:

(1) To recognize and declare that the opportunity to obtain employment, labor union membership, housing accommodations, property rights, education, public accommodations and public services without discrimination based on race, color, creed, religion, ancestry national origin, sex, including sexual harassment and pornography, affectional preference, disability, age, marital status, or status with regard to public assistance or to obtain housing accommodations without discrimination based on familial status is a civil right:

(2) To prevent and prohibit all discriminatory practices based on race, color, creed, religion, ancestry, national origin, sex, including sexual harassment and pornography, affectional preference, disability, age, marital status, or status with regard to public assistance with respect to employment, labor union membership, housing accommodations, property rights, education, public accommodations, or public services;

(3) To prevent and prohibit all discriminatory practices based on familial status with respect to housing accommodations;

(4) To prevent and prohibit all discriminatory practices of sexual subordination or inequality through pornography;

(5) To protect all persons from unfounded charges of discriminatory practices;

(6) To eliminate existing and the development of any ghettos in the community; and

(7) To effectuate the foregoing policy by means of public information and education, mediation and conciliation, and enforcement.

Section 3. That Section 139.20 of the above-entitled ordinance be amended by adding thereto a new subsection (gg) to read as follows: (gg) *Pornography*. Pornography is a form of discrimination on the basis of sex.

(1) Pornography is the sexually explicit subordination of women, graphically depicted, whether in pictures or in words, that also includes one or more of the following:

i) women are presented dehumanized as sexual objects,things or commodities; or

ii) women are presented as sexual objects who enjoy pain or humiliation: or

iii) women are presented as sexual objects who experience sexual pleasure in being raped; or

iv) women are presented as sexual objects tied up or cut up or mutilated or bruised or physically hurt; or

v) women are presented in postures of sexual submission: or

vi) women's body parts—including but not limited to vaginas, breasts, and buttocks—are exhibited, such that women are reduced to those parts; or

vii) women are presented as whores by nature; or

viii) women are presented being penetrated by objects or animals; or

ix) women are presented in scenarios of degradation, injury, abasement, torture, shown as filthy or inferior, bleeding, bruised, or hurt in a context that makes these conditions sexual

(2) The use of men, children, or transsexuals in the place of women in (1) (i-ix) above is pornography for purposes of subsections (1)-(p) of this statute.

Section 4. That Section 139.40 of the above-entitled ordinance be amended by adding thereto new subsections (1), (m), (n), (o), (p), (q), (r), and (s) to read as follows:

(1) *Discrimination by trafficking in pornography*. The production, sale, exhibition, or distribution of pornography is discrimination against women by means of trafficking in pornography.

(1) City, state, and federally funded public libraries or private and public university and college libraries in which pornography is available for study, including on open shelves, shall not be construed to be trafficking in pornography but special display presentations of pornography in said places is sex discrimination.

(2) The formation of private clubs or associations for purposes of trafficking in pornography is illegal and shall be considered a conspiracy to violate the civil rights of women.

(3) Any woman has cause of action hereunder as a woman acting against the subordination of women. Any man or transsexual who alleges injury by pornography in the way women are injured by it shall also have a cause of action.

(m) *Coercion into pornographic performances*. Any person, including transsexual, who is coerced, intimidated, or fraudulently induced (hereafter, "coerced") into performing for pornography shall have a cause of action against the maker(s), seller(s), exhibitor(s) or distributor(s) of said pornography for damages and for the elimination of the products of the performance(s) from the public view.

(1) *Limitation of action*. This claim shall not expire before five years have elapsed from the date of the coerced performance(s) or from the last appearance or sale of any product of the performance(s), whichever date is later;

(2) Proof of one or more of the following facts or conditions shall not, without more, negate a finding of coercion;

(i) that the person is a woman; or

(ii) that the person is or has been a prostitute; or

(iii) that the person has attained the age of majority; or

(iv) that the person is connected by blood or marriage to anyone involved in or related to the making of the pornography; or

(v) That the person has previously had, or been thought to have had, sexual relations with anyone, including anyone involved in or related to the making of the pornography; or

(vi) that the person has previously posed for sexually explicit pictures for or with anyone, including anyone involved in or related to the making of the pornography at issue; or

(vii) that anyone else, including a spouse or other relative, has given permission on the person's behalf; or

(viii) that the person actually consented to a use of the performance that is changed into pornography; or

(ix) that the person knew that the purpose of the acts or events in question was to make pornography; or

(x) that the person showed no resistance or appeared to cooperate actively in the photographic sessions or in the sexual events that produced the pornography; or

(xi) that the person signed a contract, or made statements affirming a willingness to cooperate in the production of pornography; or

(xii) that no physical force, threats, or weapons were used in the making of the pornography; or

(xiii) that the person was paid or otherwise compensated.

(n) *Forcing pornography on a person.* Any woman, man, child, or transsexual who has pornography forced on him/her in any place of employment, in education, in a home, or in any public place has a cause of action against the perpetrator and/or institution.

(o) *Assault or physical attack due to pornography.* Any woman, man, child, or transsexual who is assaulted, physically attacked or injured in a way that is directly caused by specific pornography has a claim for damages against the perpetrator, the maker(s), distributor(s), seller(s), and/or exhibitor(s), and for an injunction against the specific pornography's further exhibition, distribution, or sale. No damages shall be assessed (A) against maker(s) for pornography made, (B) against distributor(s) for pornography distributed, (C) against seller(s) for pornography sold, or (D) against exhibitors for pornography exhibited prior to the ENFORCEMENT date of this act.

(p) *Defenses.* Where the materials which are the subject matter of a cause of action under subsections (l), (m), (n), or (o) of this section are pornography, it shall not be a defense that the defendant did not know or intend that the materials were pornography or sex discrimination.

(q) *Severability.* Should any part(s) of this ordinance be found legally invalid, the remaining part(s) remain valid.

(r) Subsections (l), (m), (n) and (o) of this section are exceptions to the second clause of section 141.90 of this title.

(s) *Effective date.* Enforcement of this ordinance of December 30, 1983, shall be suspended until July 1, 1984 ("enforcement date") to facilitate training, education, voluntary compliance, and implementation taking into consideration the opinions of the City Attorney and the Civil Rights Commission. No liability shall attach under (l) or as specifically provided in the second sentence of (o) until the enforcement date. Liability under all other sections of this act shall attach as of December 30, 1983.

9. Infra note 7 at p. 633.
10. 598 F Supp 1316 (SD Ind., 1984).
11.

City-County General Ordinance No. 35, 1984, sec. 2,
amending the Code of Indianapolis and Marion County, Indiana,
Ch. 16, Human Relations; Equal Opportunity, sec. 16–3,
Definitions, subd. (q):

(q) Pornography shall mean the graphic sexually explicit subordination of women, whether in pictures or words, that also includes one or more of the following:

(1) Women are presented as sexual objects who enjoy pain or humiliation; or

(2) Women are presented as sexual objects who experience sexual pleasure in being raped; or

(3) Women are presented as sexual objects tied up or mutilated or bruised or physically hurt, or as dismembered or truncated or fragmented or severed into body parts; or

(4) Women are presented being penetrated by objects or animals; or

(5) Women are presented in scenarios of degradation, injury, abasement, torture, shown as filthy or inferior, bleeding, bruised, or hurt in a context that makes these conditions sexual;

(6) Women are presented as sexual objects for domination, conquest, violation, exploitation, possession, or use, or through postures or positions of servility or submission or display.

The use of men, children, or transsexuals in the place of women in paragraphs (1) through (6) above shall also constitute pornography under this section.

12. See section 10.3.

13. See Gertz v. Robert Welch, Inc., 418 US 323 (1974).

14. See Brandeburg v. Ohio, 395 US 444 (1969).

15. See New York v. Ferber, 458 US 747 (1982).

16. Infra note 10 at p. 1332.

17. Infra note 6 at pp. 419-20.

18. 380 US 51 (1965).

19. 771 F2d 323 (7th Cir., 1985).

20. 54 USLW 3560 (February 24, 1986).

21. See generally 20 New Eng L Rev 4 (1984-1985) at pp. 632-33.

22. 732 P2d 9 (Ore., 1987) cert den 55 USLW 2444 (1987). Also see New York Times (April 15, 1987) at p. A23.

23. 480 NE2d 1089 (N.Y., 1986), cert den 1065 CT 3172 (1986).

24. 106 S Ct 3172 (1986).

25. Infra note 7 at p. 642.

26. See Dworkin, Pornography: Men Possessing Women (1981) at p. 224; also 10 Archives of Sexual Behavior 33 (1961), and 17 J Res Personality 315 (1983).

27. 458 US 747 (1982).

28. Id. at p. 763.

29. 105 S Ct 2794 (1985).

30. 380 US 51 (1965).

31. See 37 Syracuse L Rev 977 at pp. 982-83.

32. 283 US 697 (1931).

33. 272 US 365 (1926).

34. Id. at p. 395.

35. 106 S Ct 925 (1986).

36. 748 F2d 527 (9th Cir., 1984).

37. See generally 7 Pace L Rev 251 (1986).

38. See section 2.1 herein.

39. Infra note 35 at p. 928.

40. Id. at pp. 931-32.

41. Id. at p. 934.

42. 452 US 640 (1981).

43. Infra note 35 at p. 937.
44. Id.
45. Infra note 37 at p. 265.
46. 128 Cal Rptr 363 (1976).
47. 467 F Supp 366 (SDNY 1979), aff 604 F2d 200 (2d Cir., 1979).
48. Id. at p. 206.
49. See 65 BU L Rev 923 (1985) at pp. 949-50.
50. See chapter 3.
51. Infra note 31 at pp. 998-99.
52. See people v. Hassil, 173 NE 355 (Ill., 1930).
53. 409 NYS2d 349 (1978).
54. Ala Code, sec 13-12-110 to 13A-12-113 (1977); Alas Stat, sec 11.66.100 to .150 (1962); Ky Rev Stat sec 529.020 to .070 (1975); La Rev Stat Ann, sec 14.82-.86 (1965); Md Crim Law Code, sec 27.15 (1975); Nev Rev Stat, sec 201.295 (1979); N.D. Cent Code, sec 12/29-.03 (1973); and S.D. Cod Laws Ann, sec 27-23-1 (1979).
55. Infra note 31 at p. 1001.
56. 3 QB 360 (1868).
57. 354 US 476 (1957).
58. Id. at p. 487. According to the court,

The dispositive question is whether obscenity is utterance within the area of protected speech and press. Although this is the first time the question has been squarely presented to this Court either under the First Amendment or under the Fourtenth Amendment, expressions found in numerous opinions indicate that this Court has always assumed that obscenity is not protected by the freedoms of speech and press.

The guaranties of freedom of expression in effect in 10 of the 14 States which by 1792 had ratified the Constitution, gave no absolute protection for every utterance. Thirteen of the 17 States provided for the prosecution of libel, and all of those States made either blasphemy or profanity, or both, statutory crimes. As early as 1712, Massachusetts made it criminal to publish "any filthy, obscene, or profane song, pamphlet, libel or mock sermon" in imitation or mimicking of religious services. . . .

In light of this history, it is apparent that the unconditional phrasing of the First Amendment was not intended to protect every utterance. This phrasing did not prevent this Court from concluding that libelous utterances are not within the area of constitutionally protected speech. *Beauharnais v. Illinois.* At the time of the adoption of the First Amendment, obscenity law was not as fully developed as libel law, but there is sufficiently contemporaneous evidence to show that obscenity, too, was outside the protection intended for speech and press.

The protection given speech and press was fashioned to assure unfettered interchange of ideas for the bringing about of political and social changes desired by the people. . . .

The Roth court concluded:

We hold that obscenity is not within the area of constitutionally protected speech or press.

It is strenuously urged that these obscenity statutes offend the constitutional guaranties because they punish incitation to impure sexual *thoughts,* not shown to be related to any overt antisocial conduct which is or may be incited in the persons stimulated to such *thoughts.* In *Roth,* the trial judge instructed the jury: "The words 'obscene, lewd and lascivious' as used in the law, signify that form of immorality which has relation to sexual impurity and has a tendency to excite lustful *thoughts.*" (Emphasis added.) In *Alberts,* the trial judge applied the

[test] whether the material has "a substantial tendency to deprave or corrupt its readers by inciting lascivious *thoughts* or arousing lustful desires." (Emphasis added.) It is insisted that the constitutional guaranties are violated because convictions may be had without proof either that obscene material will perceptibly create a clear and present danger of antisocial conduct, or will probably induce its recipients to such conduct. But, in light of our holding that obscenity is not protected speech, the complete answer to this argument is in the holding of this Court in *Beauharnais*:

"Libelous utterances not being within the area of constitutionally protected speech, it is unnecessary, either for us or for the State courts, to consider the issues behind the phrase 'clear and present danger.' Certainly no one would contend that obscene speech, for example, may be punished only upon a showing of such circumstances. Libel, as we have seen, is in the same class."

However, sex and obscenity are not synonymous. Obscene material is material which deals with sex in a manner appealing to prurient interest. The portrayal of sex, e.g., in art, literature and scientific works, is not itself sufficient reason to deny material the constitutional protection of freedom of speech and press. Sex, a great and mysterious motive force in human life, has indisputably been a subject of absorbing interest to mankind through the ages; it is one of the vital problems of human interest and public concern. . . .

The fundamental freedoms of speech and press have contributed greatly to the development and well-being of our free society and are indispensable to its continued growth. Ceaseless vigilance is the watchword to prevent their erosion by Congress or by the States. The door barring federal and state intrusion into this area cannot be left ajar; it must be kept tightly closed and opened only the slightest crack necessary to prevent encroachment upon more important interests. It is therefore vital that the standards for judging obscenity safeguard the protection of freedom of speech and press for material which does not treat sex in a manner appealing to prurient interest.

59. The dissent of Justice Harlan took a limited view of federal power over obscenity:

The danger is perhaps not great if the people of one State, through their legislature, decide that "Lady Chatterley's Lover" goes so far beyond the acceptable standards of candor that it will be deemed offensive and nonsellable, for the State next door is still free to make its own choice. At least we do not have one uniform standard. But the dangers to free thought and expression are truly great if the Federal Government imposes a blanket ban over the Nation on such a book. The prerogative of the States to differ on their ideas of morality will be destroyed, the ability of States to experiment will be stunted. The fact that the people of one State cannot read some of the works of D. H. Lawrence seems to me, if not wise or desirable, at least acceptable. But that no person in the United States should be allowed to do so seems to me intolerable, and violative of both the letter and spirit of the First Amendment. . . . So viewed, I do not think that this conviction can be upheld. The petitioner was convicted under a statute which, under the judge's charge, makes it criminal to sell books which "tend to stir sexual impulses and lead to sexually impure thoughts." I cannot agree that any book which tends to stir sexual impulses and lead to sexually impure thoughts necessarily is "utterly without redeeming social importance." Not only did this charge fail to measure up to the standards which I understand the Court to approve, but as far as I can see, much of the great literature of the world could lead to conviction under such a view of the statute. Moreover, in no event do I think that the limited federal interest in this area can extend to mere "thoughts." The Federal Government has no business, whether under the postal or commerce power, to bar the sale of books because they might lead to any kind of "thoughts."

It is no answer to say, as the Court does, that obscenity is not protected speech. The point is that this statute, as here construed, defines obscenity so widely that it encompasses matters which might very well be protected speech. I do not think that the federal statute can be constitutionally construed to reach other than what the Government has termed as "hard-core" pornography.

(2d. at 502 et seq)
The dissent of Justice Douglas (joined in by Justice Black) asserted:

When we sustain these convictions, we make the legality of a publication turn on the purity of thought which a book or tract instills in the mind of the reader. I do not think we can approve that standard and be faithful to the command of the First Amendment. . . .

The tests by which these convictions were obtained require only the arousing of sexual thoughts. Yet the arousing of sexual thoughts and desires happens every day in normal life in dozens of ways. Nearly 30 years ago a questionnaire sent to college and normal school women graduates asked what things were most stimulating sexually. Of 409 replies, 9 said "music"; 18 said "pictures"; 29 said "dancing"; 40 said "drama"; 95 said "books"; and 218 said "man." Alpert, *Judicial Censorship of Obscene Literature,* 52 Harv.L.Rev. 40, 73.

The test of obscenity the Court endorses today gives the censor free range over a vast domain. To allow the State to step in and punish mere speech or publication that the judge or the jury thinks has an *undesirable* impact on thoughts but that is not shown to be a part of unlawful action is drastically to curtail the First Amendment. As recently stated by two of our outstanding authorities on obscenity, "The danger of influencing a change in the current moral standards of the community, or of shocking or offending readers, or of stimulating sex thoughts or desires apart from objective conduct, can never justify the losses to society that result from interference with literary freedom." Lockhart & McClure, *Literature, The Law of Obscenity and the Constitution,* 38 Minn.L.Rev. 295, 387.

If we were certain that impurity of sexual thoughts impelled to action, we would be on less dangerous ground in punishing the distributors of this sex literature. But it is by no means clear that obscene literature, as so defined, is a significant factor in influencing substantial deviations from the community standards. . . .

The absence of dependable information on the effect of obscene literature on human conduct should make us wary. It should put us on the side of protecting society's interest in literature, except and unless it can be said that the particular publication has an impact on action that the government can control.

60. Id. at p. 489.
61. 413 US 49 (1973) at p. 103.
62. 413 US 15 (1973):

Under a national Constitution, fundamental First Amendment limitations on the powers of the States do not vary from community to community, but this does not mean that there are, or should or can be, fixed, uniform national standards of precisely what appeals to the "prurient interest" or is "patently offensive." These are essentially questions of fact, and our nation is simply too big and too diverse for this Court to reasonably expect that such standards could be articulated for all 50 States in a single formulation, even assuming the prerequisite consensus exists. When triers of fact are asked to decide whether "the average person, applying contemporary community standards" would consider certain materials "prurient,"it would be unrealistic to require that the answer be based on some abstract formulation. The adversary system, with lay jurors as the usual ultimate factfinders in criminal prosecutions, has historically permitted triers-of-fact to draw on the standards of their community, guided always by limiting instructions on the law. To require a State to structure obscenity proceedings around evidence of a *national* "community standard" would be an exercise in futility. . . .

We conclude that neither the State's alleged failure to offer evidence of "national standards," nor the trial court's charge that the jury consider state community standards, were constitutional errors. Nothing in the First Amendment requires that a jury must consider hypothetical and unascertainable "national standards" when attempting to determine whether certain materials are obscene as a matter of fact. . . .

[I]n our view, to equate the free and robust exchange of ideas and political debate with commercial exploitation of obscene material demeans the grand conception of the First Amendment and its high purposes in the historic struggle for freedom. [The] First Amendment protects works which, taken as a whole, have serious literary, artistic, political or scientific value, regardless of whether the government or a majority of the people approve of the ideas these works represent. "The protection given speech and press was fashioned to assure unfettered interchange of *ideas* for the bringing about of political and social changes desired by the people. . . . But the public portrayal of hard core sexual conduct for its own sake, and for the ensuing commercial gain, is a different matter.

There is no evidence empirical or historical, that the stern 19th century American censorship of public distribution and display of material relating to sex in any way limited or affected expression of serious literary, artistic, political, or scientific ideas. On the contrary, it is beyond any question that the era following Thomas Jefferson to Theodore Roosevelt was an "extraordinarily vigorous period" not just in economics and politics, but in *belles lettres* and in "the outlying fields of social and political philosophies." We do not see the harsh hand of censorship of ideas—good or bad, sound or unsound—and "repression" of political liberty lurking in every state regulation of commercial exploitation of human interest in sex.

If a specific book, play, paper, or motion picture has in a civil proceeding been condemned as obscene and review of that finding has been completed, and thereafter a person publishes, shows, or displays that particular book or film, then a vague law has been made specific. There would remain the underlying question whether the First Amendment allows an implied exception in the case of obscenity. I do not think it does and my views on the issue have been stated over and again. But at least a criminal prosecution brought at that juncture would not violate the time-honored void-for-vagueness test.

No such protective procedure has been designed by California in this case. Obscenity—which even we cannot define with precision—is a hodge-podge. To send men to jail for violating standards they cannot understand, construe, and apply is a monstrous thing to do in a Nation dedicated to fair trials and due process.

The idea that the First Amendment permits government to ban publications that are "offensive" to some people puts an ominous gloss on freedom of the press. [The] First Amendment was designed "to invite dispute," to induce "a condition of unrest," to "create dissatisfactions with conditions as they are," and even to stir "people to anger." . . . The idea that the First Amendment permits punishment for ideas that are "offensive" to the particular judge or jury sitting in judgment is astounding. No greater leveler of speech or literature has ever been designed.

63. Infra note 57.

64. Infra note 62 at p. 24.

65. See United States v. Various Articles of Obscene Material, 709 F2d 132 (2d Cir., 1983) at pp. 135-36.

66. 461 NE2d 744 Ind. App., 1984).

67. Infra note 57.

68. Infra note 62.

69. 418 US 153 (1974).

70. 405 US 438 (1971).

71. 55 USLW 4595 (1987). According to the Court,

The question remains whether the convictions should be reversed outright or are subject to salvage if the erroneous instruction is found to be harmless error. Petitioners contend that the statute is invalid on its face and that the convictions must necessarily be reversed because, as we understand it, the State should not be allowed to preserve any conviction under a law that poses a threat to First Amendment values. But the statute under which petitioners were convicted is no longer on the books; it has been repealed and replaced by a statute that does not call for the application of community standards to the value question. Facial invalidation of the repealed statute would not serve the purpose of preventing future prosecutions under a constitutionally defective standard. Cf., *e.g., Secretary of State of Maryland v. Joseph H. Munson Co.,* 467 U.S. 947, 964-968, and n. 13 (1984). And if we did facially invalidate the repealed statute and reverse petitioners' convictions, petitioners could still be retried under that statute, provided that the erroneous instruction was not repeated, because petitioners could not plausibly claim that the repealed statute failed to give them notice that the sale of obscene materials would be prosecuted. See *Dombrowski v. Pfister,* 380 U.S. 479, 491, n 7 (1965); *United States v. Thirty-Seven Photographs,* 402 U.S. 363, 375, n. 3 (1971). Under these circumstances, we see no reason to require a retrial if it can be said beyond a reasonable doubt that the jury's verdict in this case was not affected by the erroneous instruction.

The situation here is comparable to that in *Rose v. Clark,* 478 U.S.——(1986). In *Rose,* the jury in a murder trial was incorrectly instructed on the element of malice, yet the Court held that a harmless error inquiry was appropriate. The Court explained that in the absence of error that renders a trial fundamentally unfair, such as denial of the right to counsel or trial before a financially interested judge, a conviction should be affirmed "where a reviewing court can find that the record developed at trial established guilt beyond a reasonable doubt. . . . " *Id.,* at——. The error in *Rose* did not entirely preclude the jury from considering the element of malice, *id.,* at——, n. 8, and the fact that the jury could conceivably have had the impermissible presumption in mind when it considered the element of malice was not a reason to retry the defendant if the facts that the jury necessarily found established guilt beyond a reasonable doubt. The Court said, "When a jury is instructed to presume malice from predicate facts, it still must find the existence of those facts beyond reasonable doubt. *Connecticut v. Johnson,* 460 U.S. 73, 96-97 (1983) (Powell, J., dissenting). In many cases, the predicate facts conclusively establish intent, so that no rational jury could find that the defendant committed the relevant criminal act but did not *intend* to cause injury." *Id.,* at——.

Similarly, in the present cases the jurors were not precluded from considering the question of value: they were informed that to convict they must find, among other things, that the magazines petitioners sold were utterly without redeeming social value. While it was error to instruct the juries to use a state community standard in considering the value question, if a reviewing court concludes that no rational juror, if properly instructed, could find value in the magazines, the convictions should stand.

Although we plainly have the authority to decide whether, on the facts of a given case, a constitutional error was harmless under the standard of *Chapman v. California,* 386 U.S. 18 (1967), we do so sparingly. *Rose v. Clark,* supra, at——In this case the Illinois Court of Appeals has not considered the harmless-error issue. We therefore vacate its judgment and remand so that it may do so.

The dissent of Justice Stevens with whom Justice Marshall joined emphasized that the majority opinion's

attempt to clarify the constitutional definition of obscenity is not faithful to the First Amendment . . . communicative material of this sort is entitled to the protection of the First Amendment if *some reasonable persons* could consider it as having serious literary artistic, political, or scientific value. Over 40 years ago, the Court recognized that

"Under our system of government there is an accommodation for the widest varieties of tastes and ideas. What is good literature, what has educational value, what is refined public information, what is good art, varies with individuals as it does from one generation to another. . . . From the multitude of competing offerings the public will pick and choose. What seems to one to be trash may have for others fleeting or even enduring values." *Hannegan v. Esquire, Inc.,* 327 U.S. 146, 157 (1946).

The purpose of the third element of the *Miller* test is to ensure that the obscenity laws not be allowed to " 'level' the available reading matter to the majority or lowest common denominator of the population. . . . It is obvious that neither *Ulysses* nor *Lady Chatterley's Lover* would have literary appeal to the majority of the population." F. Schauer, The Law of Obscenity 144 (1976). A juror asked to create "a reasonable person" in order to apply the standard that the Court announces today, might well believe that the majority of the population who find no value in such a book are more reasonable than the minority who do find value. First Amendment protection surely must not be contingent on this type of subjective determination.

72. Infra note 62.

It should be noted that in 1967 Congress had created the Commission on Obscenity and Pornography and had directed the Commission to "study the effect of pornography and obscenity upon the public, and particularly minor, and its relationship to other antisocial behavior." 18 USC 1461 (1967) The Report of the Commission (1970) concluded as follows:

"In general, established patterns of sexual behavior were found to be very stable and not altered substantially by exposure to erotica. When sexual activity occurred following the viewing or reading of these materials, it constituted temporary activation of individuals' preexisting patterns of sexual behavior."(p. 25)

"Exposure to erotic stimuli appears to have little or no effect on already established attitudinal commitments regarding either sexuality or sexual morality."(p. 26)

"Research to date . . . provides no substantial basis for the belief that erotic materials constitute a primary or significant cause of the development of character deficits or that they operate as a significant determinative factor in causing crime and delinquency.

"This conclusion is stated with due and perhaps excessive caution, since it is obviously not possible, and never would be possible to state that never on any occasion, under any conditions, did any erotic material ever contribute in any way to the likelihood of any individual committing a sex crime. Indeed, no such statement could be made about any kind of non-erotic material. On the basis of the available data, however, it is not possible to conclude that erotic material is a significant cause of sex crime."(p. 243)

For critical comment on the report, see Lockhart, *The Findings and Recommendations of the Commission on Obscenity and Pornography,* 24 Okla.L.Rev. 209 (1971); Clor, *Science, Eros & the Law: A Critique of the Obscenity Commission Report,* 10 Duq.L.Rev. 63 (1971); Johnson, *The Pornography Report: Epistemology, Methodology, & Ideology,* 10 Duq.L.Rev. 190 (1971).

In support of the report, note A Book Named "John Cleland's Memoirs of a Woman of Pleasure" v. Attorney General 383 US 413, 86 S Ct 975 (1966) in which Justice Brennan, writing the majority opinion, pointed out at the onset of his opinion that

This is an obscenity case in which *Memoirs of a Woman of Pleasure* (commonly known as *Fanny Hill*), written by John Cleland in about 1750, was adjudged obscene in a proceeding that put on trial the book itself, and not its publisher or distributor. [At] the hearing [the] court received the book in evidence, . . . heard the testimony of experts and accepted other evidence, such as book reviews, in order to assess the literary, cultural, or educational character of the book. This constituted the entire evidence. . . . The trial justice . . . adjudged

Memoirs obscene and declared that the book "is not entitled to the protection of the First and Fourteenth amendments. . . . The Massachusetts Supreme Judicial Court affirmed. We reverse.

[T]he sole question before the state courts was whether *Memoirs* satisfies the test of obscenity established in *Roth* [under whose definition of obscenity], as elaborated in subsequent cases, three elements must coalesce: it must be established that (a) the dominant theme of the material taken as a whole appeals to a prurient interest in sex; (b) the material is patently offensive because it affronts contemporary community standards relating to the description or representation of sexual matters; and (c) the material is utterly without redeeming social value.

The Supreme Judicial Court purported to apply the *Roth* definition of obscenity and held all three criteria satisfied. We need not consider the claim that the court erred in concluding that *Memoirs* satisfied the prurient appeal and patent offensiveness criteria; for reversal is required because the court misinterpreted the social value criterion.

The Supreme Judicial Court erred in holding that a book need not be "unqualifiedly worthless before it can be deemed obscene." A book can not be proscribed unless it is found to be *utterly* without redeeming social value. This is so even though the book is found to possess the requisite prurient appeal and to be patently offensive. Each of the three federal constitutional criteria is to be applied independently; the social value of the book can neither be weighed against nor canceled by its prurient appeal or patent offensiveness. Hence, even on the view of the court below that *Memoirs* possessed only a modicum of social value, its judgment must be reversed as being founded on an erroneous interpretation of a federal constitutional standard.

It does not necessarily follow from this reversal that a determination that *Memoirs* is obscene in the constitutional sense would be improper under all circumstances. On the premise, which we have no occasion to assess, the *Memoirs* has the requisite prurient appeal and is patently offensive, but has only a minimum of social value, the circumstances of production, sale, and publicity are relevant in determining whether or not the publication and distribution of the book is constitutionally protected. Evidence that the book was commercially exploited for the sake of prurient appeal, to the exclusion of all other values, might justify the conclusion that the book was utterly without redeeming social importance. It is not that in such a setting the social value test is relaxed so as to dispense with the requirement that a book be *utterly* devoid of social value, but rather that, as we elaborate in *Ginzburg v. United States,* where the purveyor's sole emphasis is on the sexually provocative aspects of his publications, a court could accept his evaluation at its face value. In this proceeding, however, the courts were asked to judge the obscenity of *Memoirs* in the abstract. . . . All possible uses of the book must therefore be considered, and the mere risk that the book might be exploited by panderers because it so pervasively treats sexual matters cannot alter the fact—given the view of the Massachusetts court attributing to *Memoirs* a modicum of literary and historical value—that the book will have redeeming social importance in the hands of those who publish or distribute it on the basis of that value.

The dissent of Justice Clark was simply expressed:

I have "stomached" past cases for almost 10 years without much outcry. Though I am not known to be a purist—or a shrinking violet—this book is too much even for me. . . .

While there is no majority opinion in this case [three Justices] import a new test into that laid down in *Roth,* namely, that "a book cannot be proscribed unless it is found to be utterly without redeeming social value." . . .

In my view evidence of social importance is relevant to the determination of the ultimate question of obscenity. But social importance does not constitute a separate and distinct constitutional test. Such evidence must be considered together with evidence that the material in question appeals to prurient interest and is patently offensive. . . .

Memoirs is nothing more than a series of minutely and vividly described sexual episodes. [There] can be no doubt that the whole purpose of the book is to arouse the prurient interest. Likewise the repetition of sexual episode after episode and the candor with which they are described renders the book "patently offensive." These facts weigh heavily in any appraisal of the book's claims to "redeeming social importance."

[If] a book deals solely with erotic material in a manner calculated to appeal to the prurient interest, it matters not that it may be expressed in beautiful prose. There are obviously dynamic connections between art and sex—the emotional, intellectual, and physical—but where the former is used solely to promote prurient appeal, it cannot claim constitutional immunity. . . . In my view, the book's repeated and unrelieved appeals to the prurient interest of the average person leave it utterly without redeeming social importance.

73. See People v. Doubleday & Co., 71 NYS2d 736 (1947), aff 77 NE2d 6 (N.Y., 1947), aff 335 US 848 (1948).

74. See Commonwealth of Pennsylvania v. Gordon, 66 Pa D & C 101 (1949), aff 70 A2d 389 (Pa., 1950).

75. See Hannegan v. Esquire, Inc., 327 US 146 (1946).

76. Infra note 57 at p. 484.

77. 394 US 557 (1969).

78. 81 Yale L J xx (1971) at pp. 328-29.

79. People v. Dial Press, Inc., 48 NYS2d 480 (1944).

80. Commonwealth v. Isenstadt, 62 NE2d 840 (Mass., 1945).

81. 749 F2d 113 (2d Cir., 1984).

82. Id. at p. 121.

83. Id. p. 6.

84. Id.

85. 98 S Ct 3026 (1978). See also Tribe, American Constitutional Law (1978), Chapter 12.

86. The "seven dirty words" Carlin spoke were fuck, shit, piss, motherfucker, cocksucker, cunt, and tit.

87. "New Indecency Enforcement Standards To Be Applied to All Broadcast and Amateur Radio Licensees," Public Notice, FCC 87-153 (released April 29, 1987).

88. Id. at p. 2.

89. 506 NYS2d, 869 (1986).

90. 408 US 104, 92 S Ct 2294 (1972).

91. Id. at p. 120.

92. 106 S Ct 3159 (1986).

93. See 2 Conn J of Internat L 509 (1987) at pp. 523-24.

94. Infra note 92.

95. 315 US 568, 62 S Ct 766 (1942).

96. 310 US 296, 60 S Ct 900 (1940).

97. Utah Code Ann Sections 76-10-1071 to -1708 (1983).

98. Section 76-10-1702(4)(d) of the act.

99. See Community Television of Utah, Inc. v. Wilkinson, 611 F Supp 1099 (Utah, 1985).

100. 800 F2d 989 (10th Cir., 1986).

101. Id. at p. 990.

102. 438 US 726 (1978).

103. 107 S Ct 1559 (1987).

104. See Abrams, "Cable Television and 'Indecency': The Free-Speech Battle Continues," NLJ (July 13, 1987) at 18 et seq.

105. 531 F Supp 987 (Utah, 1982).

106. 555 F Supp 1164 (Utah, 1982).

107. 755 F2d 1415 (11th Cir., 1985).

108. Infra note 104 at 19.

109. 106 S Ct 2034 (1986).

110. 660 F2d 1370 (10th Cir., 1981), cert dism 456 US 1001 (1982).

111. See generally Robertson & Nicol, Media Law: The Rights of Journalists, Broadcasters and Publishers (Sage Publications, 1984) at chapter 3.

112. Section 1(3)(b) of both acts.

113. Infra note 100 86 at p. 75.

114. See Attorney-General's Ref No. 5 of 1980, (1980) 3 ALL ER 816.

115. (1976) Crim L R 514.

116. No. 76 (HMSO 1976), ch 3, paragraphs 69–76.

117. Infra note 111 at p. 77.

118. See Hensher Ltd. v. Restawile Upholstery Ltd. (1976) A.C. 64.

119. (1977) A.C. 699.

120. Infra note 96 at p. 65.

121. (1962) 1 QB 163.

122. (1973) A.C. 435.

123. Id. at p. 495.

124. (1968) Crim L R 503.

125. (1978) 68 Crim App R at p. 82.

126. See Regina v. Holbrook (1978), 4 QBD 42.

127. At 1 et seq.

Selected Bibliography

Chafee, Free Speech in the United States (1941).
Meiklejohn, Alexander. Political Freedom: The Constitutional Powers of the People (1948).
Note, 40 Harv L Rev 153 (1926).
Note, 27 U Chi L Rev 315 (1960).
Note, 37 NYU L Rev 181 (1962).
Note, 116 U Pa L Rev 975 (1968).
Note, 40 U Chi L Rev 235 (1973).
Note, 122 U Pa L Rev 1071 (1974).
Note, 88 Harv L Rev 1482 (1975).
Note, 7 Hastings Const L Q 579 (1980).
Note, 34 U Miami L Rev 793 (1980).
Note, 25 Wm & Mary L Rev 189 (1983).
Note, 82 Mich L Rev 1447 (1984).
Note, 100 Harv L Rev 100 (1986) at 172.
Note, 7 Pace L Rev 251 (1986).
Note, 2 Conn J Int'l L 509 (1987).
Note, 19 Conn L Rev 561 (1987).
Note, J Law & Pol, vol 3, 625 (Spring 1987).
Tribe, Laurence H. American Constitutional Law (1978) at 673 et seq.
Warner, Radio and Television Law (1948).

IMPORTANT NOTES AND ARTICLES

26 Loy L Rev 739 (1980).
90 Yale L J 165 (1980).
5 U Haw L Rev 79 (1981).
46 Alb L Rev 1501 (1982).
95 Harv L Rev 1324 (1982).
6 U Haw L Rev 693 (1983).

30 Wayne L Rev 93 (1983).
33 U Kan L Rev 305 (1985).
8 U Puget Sound L Rev 157 (1985).
90 Dick L Rev 705 (1986).
35 Emory L J 59 (1986).
9 Harv J L & Pub Pol'y 760 (1986).
71 Iowa L Rev 2405 (1986).
59 S Cal L Rev 1227 (1986).
30 Wash U J Urb & Contemp L 333 (1986).

Index to Cases

Subject Index

About the Author

WARREN FREEDMAN, now retired, was Counsel for Bristol-Myers Company. He taught at Rutgers University School of Law and the New School for Social Research. His numerous works on legal topics include *The Right of Privacy in the Computer Age, Frivolous Lawsuits and Frivolous Defenses, Federal Statutes on Environmental Protection,* and *Professional Sports and Antitrust,* all published by Quorum Books.